THE SAINTS PRAY FOR YOU

THE
SAINTS
PRAY
FOR YOU

HOW THE CHRISTIANS IN HEAVEN
HELP US HERE ON EARTH

BY KARLO BROUSSARD

Catholic
Answers
Press

Published by Catholic Answers, Inc.
2020 Gillespie Way
El Cajon, California 92020
1-888-291-8000 orders
619-387-0042 fax
catholic.com

Printed in the United States of America

Cover design by ebooklaunch.com
Interior design by Maria Bowman

978-1-68357-359-3
978-1-68357-360-9 Kindle
978-1-68357-361-6 ePub

I'd like to dedicate this book to
Mother Mary Angelica of the Resurrection.

Mother Angelica, pray for us!

Contents

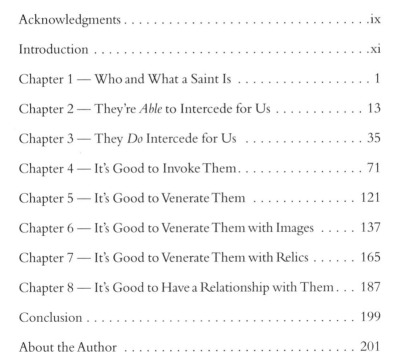

Acknowledgments

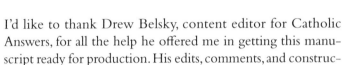

I'd like to thank Drew Belsky, content editor for Catholic Answers, for all the help he offered me in getting this manuscript ready for production. His edits, comments, and constructive critical suggestions never fail to make for a better book to be read. May all the patron saints of editors intercede for him in his work at Catholic Answers.

Introduction

After the doctrines surrounding the Virgin Mary, the Catholic doctrine of the intercession of the saints, and the practices associated with it—our *invocation* (asking for help) and *veneration* (acts of honor) of them—may elicit more challenges from non-Catholic Christians (excluding the Orthodox, who agree with us on the saints) than any other topic. In fact, Mary's often the gateway to this doctrine. "Why do Catholics worship Mary?" it's often asked. "Why go to Mary when you can go straight to Jesus?"

Challenges to the invocation of the saints tend to be of two types. Some challenges are based on the idea that it's not appropriate for Christians to request that the saints pray for them: either it takes away from the uniqueness of Jesus' mediation or God outright forbids it as an "abominable practice" (Deut. 18:12). Other challenges are more practical: some Christians may think that, in principle, requesting that the saints pray for us could be appropriate, but it's futile to do so because the souls in heaven aren't able to intercede for us.

The veneration of the saints is just as much, if not more, of a concern for non-Catholic Christians. Sometimes the issue is the idea of veneration itself. Other times, it's *how* we venerate the saints—venerating their images and relics, for example. Regardless, our veneration of the saints is perceived as worship and therefore idolatry.

The Church's take on the saints can be challenging for Catholics as well. Veteran Catholics might want to know things like "Can a saint ever stop being a saint?" or "Are there non-Catholic saints?" Recent converts to Catholicism sometimes are uncomfortable with the *practice* of having a devotion to the saints, so they want to know exactly what is required of them. *Must* they have a devotion to a saint? Must they accept everything a saint writes? And then converts who are okay with the practice often want to know *how* to have a devotion to the saints.

It's important that we recognize the particular challenges to Catholic doctrine regarding the saints. In our conversations, if we know what the obstacle is, we can focus our time and attention on making an effective answer.

The motivation behind these challenges is understandable. We don't want to do anything that contradicts the Bible or takes away from Jesus. Nor do we want to engage in pointless attempts at piety. But as we meet these challenges, we'll see that these motivations are simply mistaken when it comes to our Catholic beliefs about the saints, their intercession, and the honor that we give them. These beliefs are scriptural, and they give great honor to Jesus and his saving work.

It's important that we have adequate answers to queries from Catholics as well. Catholics need to know the truth about the saints, and *all* Catholics have been called by Christ to experience the graces that can flow from having healthy relationships with those fellow Christians who are perfected in him. They are our brothers and sisters. Together, we are the "household of God" (1 Tim. 3:15).

The purpose of this book is to explain and defend Catholic beliefs and practices that relate to the saints in heaven. Chapter one covers who and what a saint is. It's important that we know *whom* we're invoking for help and showing honor to.

Chapters two and three deal with our justification of two theses that our invocation of the saints presupposes: 1) the saints are *able* to intercede for us, and 2) the saints in fact *do* intercede for us, both generally and specifically. Before we ask for the saints' help, we need to know whether they're able to help; otherwise, we'd be engaging in futile piety. Also, we need confirmation that God wills the saints in heaven to intercede for us, lest our requests be lost in a void.

Chapter four shifts to the practice of *invoking* the saints' intercession. It's one thing to say that the saints intercede for us, but it's another thing to say it's appropriate Christian piety to ask them to do so. Here we'll give justification for the thesis that it is.

The focus of the book then moves to the Christian practice of *venerating* (honoring/reverencing) the saints, again asking whether such a pious practice is appropriate for a Christian. Chapter five makes good on the thesis that it is appropriate Christian piety. Chapter six continues with the topic of veneration but zeroes in on the thesis that it's appropriate for a Christian to venerate saints by venerating *their images*, whether that be a statue, a holy medal, or an icon. Chapter seven shifts gears from images to relics, giving reasons to think it's appropriate for a Christian to venerate the saints by venerating the physical objects they have left behind for us.

Finally, in chapter eight, we turn to our relationship with the saints. How do we foster our devotion to the saints? What are some practical tips as to how we can make patron saints a part of our Christian life? Should we have relationships with multiple saints? It's these questions and more that we will answer in chapter eight.

The chapters that deal specifically with apologetical theses—chapters two, three, four, five, six, and seven—will be divided into two major parts: arguments in favor and arguments against, all of which are a mix of biblical, historical, and theological types. Our intention is to provide a fair hearing from both sides of the debate. But we conclude that the position in *favor* of these issues is the stronger.

My experience as an apologist has been that a defense of the above Catholic beliefs and practices surrounding the saints leads to conversion. A few years back, a gentleman visited Catholic Answers' headquarters to thank me for helping him and his wife into the Church from one of the Protestant traditions. With great excitement, he shared with me how the year before, he had just so happened to come across an episode of *Catholic Answers Live* where I was talking about the intercession of the saints. He explained that upon hearing me give some of the arguments in this book, he was convinced that the intercession of the saints is true. "I immediately went home and shared it with my wife," he said. "And here I am today, a Catholic. We just entered the Church this past Easter Vigil." I tell you, my friends, this stuff actually works!

As mentioned above, the saints in heaven are our brothers and sisters within "the household of God, the Church." I pray that this book will help you, and those you minister to, enjoy more fully the blessings of this great family.

CHAPTER 1

Who and What a Saint Is

Y ou can't search for something unless you first have some knowledge of what you're looking for. Similarly, you can't defend something unless you first have some knowledge of what you're defending. In this book, we're defending beliefs and practices related to the *saints*. But what do we mean by saint? *Who* are they? *Where* are they? How do you become one? It's these sorts of questions that we will address in this chapter.

What We Mean by "Saint"

The word *saint* comes from the Latin word *sanctus*, which means "holy one." The Greek equivalent *hagios* (which means "sanctified," "set apart," or "holy") is used in a variety of ways in the Bible—both the Greek version of the Old Testament (known as the *Septuagint*) and the New Testament.[1] For example,

- Christians on earth are "saints" (2 Cor. 1:1, Eph. 1:1, Col. 1:2, Phil. 1:1, Rev. 5:8).

- The Israelites are "holy" (Lev. 20:26) and, therefore, are called "saints" (Ps. 34:9; Dan. 7:18, 8:24).

- Angels are called "holy ones" (Ps. 89:6; Dan. 4:13, 17, 23, 8:13).

- A person of notable holiness is called "holy" or "saint" (Isa. 4:3-4, Matt. 27:52-53).

- Jesus is the "Holy One" of God (Mark 1:24, Luke 4:34, John 6:67-69).

- God is the "Holy One of Israel" (Ps. 71:22, 78:41, 89:18; Isa. 1:4; Jer. 50:29).

The Catholic Church uses the term *saint* in a few different ways, all of which have to do with those united to Christ. The most familiar use is with regard to those Christians who, according to the *Catechism of the Catholic Church* (CCC) in paragraph 2683, "have preceded us into the kingdom [of heaven]" *and* have their virtues publicly recognized and proclaimed when they are canonized "as saints."[2]

But the Church also extends application of the term *saint* to *every* soul united to Christ in baptism, which includes Christians on earth, souls in purgatory, and those souls in heaven who haven't been canonized. The *Catechism* explains in paragraph 1475:

> In the *communion of saints*, a perennial link of charity exists among the faithful who have already reached their heavenly home, those who are expiating their sins in purgatory, and those who are still pilgrims on earth. Among them there is, too, an abundant exchange of all good things.

The *Catechism* elsewhere states:

> After confessing "the holy Catholic Church," the Apostles' Creed adds "the communion of saints." In a certain sense this article is a further explanation of the preceding: "What is the Church if not the assembly of all the saints?" The communion of saints is the Church. . . . The term "communion of saints" therefore has two closely linked meanings: communion in holy things (*sancta*)" and "among holy persons (*sancti*) (948).

Since *saint* means "holy one," and since all baptized Christians are "holy persons" (*sancti* in Latin), set apart unto the Lord, it follows that all baptized Christians—whether on this side of the veil or the other—are "saints."

Now, it's true that Catholics don't go around calling one another Saint So-and-So. The Church typically uses the term in a narrower and more formal way for those individual Christians who are perfected in the heavenly kingdom. Why is that?

Since the blessed in heaven are perfected in righteousness, they are "saints" in the fullest sense of the term. They are completely holy, perfected by God and separated unto him. Unlike us, their saintliness is not mixed with sin and disordered inclinations. Our saintly status is a share in part of the saintly status of those in heaven. This seems to be how St. Paul describes it in Colossians 1:12: "Giving thanks to the Father, who has qualified us to share in the inheritance of the saints in light."

The Greek word for *share* in this verse is *meris*, which literally means "part or portion." It can mean to take part in the same amount, but it can also mean to take part in a lesser portion, as opposed to possessing in full. For example, Paul writes in 2 Corinthians 1:13-14, "I hope you will understand fully, as you have understood in part [Gk. *merous*], that you can be proud of us as we can be of you, on the day of the Lord Jesus."

Just as here on earth, we know only in part but will know in full at the end of time, so too we share in part in the inheritance of the saints who dwell in heaven. Because of this difference and the unique status that the "saints in light" have, it's fitting that Catholics honor them with the title *saint*.

How to Become a Saint

As we continue our inquiry as to what it means to be a saint, we need to answer the question: "How does someone *become* a saint?"

The answer depends on precisely what is meant by *saint*. If *saint* is taken to refer to simply being united to Christ (and thus a Christian), then the answer is baptism.

St. Paul teaches in 1 Corinthians 12:13, "For by one Spirit we were all *baptized into one body*—Jews or Greeks, slaves or free—and all were made to drink of one Spirit." The *one body* Paul writes of here refers to the body of Christ, as seen in verse 27. Moreover, in Romans 6:3-5, he writes:

> Do you not know that all of us who have been baptized into Christ Jesus were baptized into his death? We were buried therefore with him by baptism into death, so that as Christ was raised from the dead by the glory of the Father, we too might walk in newness of life. For if we have been united with him in a death like his, we shall certainly be united with him in a resurrection like his.

So baptism is the gate through which we are initially united to Christ and thus become *saints*, set apart unto him as members of his mystical body.

Now, to become a *saint* in the sense of entering heaven, we must, as Hebrews 4:14 says, "hold fast our confession," and, according to Jesus in Matthew 10:22, persevere in friendship with Christ unto the end of our lives. Dying in friendship with Christ guarantees entrance into the heavenly kingdom.

To become a *canonized* saint—someone whom the Church publicly declares "worthy of universal veneration"[3]—there are three stages.

The first stage involves an examination of the life of a candidate for sainthood. Phase one of the examination is at the diocesan level. The bishop of the diocese in which the person died begins the investigation into the life of the candidate at least five years after the person's death (unless the pope gives a dispensation), gathering information from witnesses establishing the candidate's martyrdom or attesting to the virtues the candidate bore witness to in his life. A candidate under investigation is given the title *servant of God*.

Phase two of the examination is carried out by the Vatican's Dicastery for the Causes of Saints, the beginning of which consists of a team of nine theologians examining the *Positio*, which is a document the Congregation prepares summarizing the evidence gathered in phase one. If the majority of the assigned theologians agree that the evidence supports the martyrdom or the virtuous life of the candidate, then the *Positio* is handed over for examination to bishops and cardinals who are members of the dicastery. If they approve, then the entire cause is given to the pope for approval. If the pope approves, he authorizes a decree declaring the candidate to be either a *venerable* (in the case that the person has lived a virtuous life) or a *blessed* (in the case that the person was martyred).

Stage two of the canonization process is called *beatification*. A decree of beatification grants permission for *limited* public veneration, usually restricted to within the boundaries of "a diocese, eparchy, region, or religious community in which the blessed lived."[4] If the candidate was martyred, then he will have been beatified already in step one, with the pope's decree. As for the candidate already declared "venerable," one miracle attributed to his intercession is required for beatification. (No miracle is required for the beatification of a martyr.) At this point, the non-martyr candidate also receives the title *blessed*.

Stage three is the actual canonization. The condition for this stage is an additional miracle attributable to the intercession of the blessed. But it must be attributed to the blessed's intercession *after* his beatification. With canonization, the individual is permitted to be publicly venerated throughout the universal Church, and he receives the formal title *saint*.

This formal process wasn't always the way things happened. For the first five centuries in the Church, instead of an official Vatican organ, it was the *vox populi* (voice of the people) that determined who was considered a saint.

Starting in the sixth century, it was the local bishop who oversaw the process of investigating the life of a person the people requested to be recognized as a saint. If the bishop approved of the person's life, he would issue a decree and thereby canonize that person.

The usual steps involved with formal canonization by the pope began in the tenth century, with Pope John XV's canonization of St. Ulric on January 31, 993, being the first recorded canonization. The rules and regulations governing the canonization of saints would be adjusted over the centuries, including adjustments made in the 1917 and 1983 *Codes of Canon Law* (CIC). The three stages described here, which come from the 1983 *Code* and new norms for the causes of canonization, are still in force today.

The Permanence of Sainthood

Now that we know how someone *becomes* a saint, the next reasonable question is whether someone can stop being a saint. There are several ways to answer.

If the question refers to whether a baptized person in this life can stop being a "saint" in the sense of no longer being fully united with the Lord, then the answer is yes. It's possible for someone to lose his status as "saint" since it's possible for someone to lose sanctifying grace in this life by committing a mortal sin. As St. Paul tells the Galatians, "You are severed from Christ, you who would be justified by the law; you have fallen away from grace" (5:4). To be severed from Christ is no longer to be in Christ, which means it's possible for the Christians in Galatia again to be subject to condemnation (Rom. 8:1—"There is no condemnation for those who are in Christ Jesus").

However, in another sense, a baptized person remains a "saint" even when he loses the state of sanctifying grace by mortal sin. The mark of baptism remains on his soul, and so he is still set apart for Jesus in this life, though he will not be saved unless he repents.

If the question refers to whether someone can stop being a saint in the sense that he loses the beatific vision in heaven, the answer here is no.

Heaven is an everlasting state of existence. The Bible speaks in many passages of heaven as "*eternal* life." In 1 Corinthians 9:25, St. Paul describes heaven as an "imperishable" wreath, implying that it never withers away. St. Peter uses the same image of an incorruptible crown in 1 Peter 5:4, writing, "When the chief Shepherd is manifested you will obtain the *unfading* crown of glory."

If the question refers to the formal status of being a canonized saint, then the question becomes, "Can the Church 'uncanonize' a saint?" The answer here is still no—at least when it comes to saints who have been canonized by the pope. A completed act of canonization by the pope is commonly taken to be irrevocable.

This is due to the fact that a solemn act of canonization is often regarded as an infallible act of the pope. In its 1998 "Doctrinal Commentary on Concluding Formula of '*Professio fidei*,'" the Congregation (now the Dicastery) for the Doctrine of the Faith (CDF, now DDF) identified the canonization of saints as an infallible act (emphasis added):

> With regard to those truths connected to revelation by historical necessity and which are to be held definitively [i.e., are infallible], but are not able to be declared as divinely revealed, the following examples can be given: the legitimacy of the election of the supreme pontiff or of the celebration of an ecumenical council, *the canonizations of saints (dogmatic facts)*, ·

the declaration of Pope Leo XIII in the Apostolic Letter *Apostolicae Curae* on the invalidity of Anglican ordinations.[5]

The infallible nature of the solemn canonization of a saint was held to be true even in the thirteenth century. St. Thomas Aquinas writes,

> Honor we show the saints is a certain profession of faith by which we believe in their glory, and it is to be piously believed that even in this the judgment of the Church is not able to err (*Quodlibet* 9:8:16).

When it comes to a person who in the past was *popularly* "canonized," and who never received official solemnization by the pope, the Church could forbid the public veneration of such a person, stating that the Church doesn't know whether he is in heaven. In this case, the Church would clarify that it never papally canonized such a person as a saint.

Now, the question often arises: "What about saints who are taken off the universal liturgical calendar, like St. Christopher? Do those people stop being saints?" The answer is no.

Removing a saint from the universal liturgical calendar is simply the Church deciding no longer to *universally* commemorate that saint on that particular day. Individual communities and Catholics can still venerate the saint who is removed from the calendar of celebrations. Religious orders, for example, venerate their own saints only within their orders. The saints on the calendar represent only a small percentage of canonized or recognized saints.

With regard to Christopher, whose feast day was removed from the universal liturgical calendar in recent decades,[6] he was never papally canonized. He was one of the early Christians who became recognized as a saint by Christian communities centuries before formal canonizations were performed by popes. However, he's still *recognized* (although not formally canonized—there was no canonization ceremony) as a saint in the Catholic Church. Catholic parishes that bear his name can still celebrate his feast day according to older calendars, and individual Catholics may continue their devotions to him.

So if we're talking about saintly status in this life, then we *can* stop being a saint. If we're talking about being a saint in heaven, whether canonized or not, then the answer is no—once a saint in heaven, always a saint.

Non-Catholics and Sainthood

Another question that sometimes comes up is, "Are there non-Catholic saints?"

The Catholic Church teaches that it's *possible* for someone who is not within the visible boundaries of the Catholic Church to be saved. The Second Vatican Council teaches the following in section 16 of its Dogmatic Constitution on the Church, *Lumen Gentium*:

> Those also can attain to salvation who through no fault of their own do not know the gospel of Christ or his Church, yet sincerely seek God and moved by grace strive by their deeds to do his will as it is known to them through the dictates of conscience. . . . Nor does divine Providence deny the helps necessary for salvation to those who, without blame on their part, have not yet arrived at an explicit knowledge of God and with his grace strive to live a good life. Whatever

good or truth is found among them is looked upon
by the Church as a preparation for the gospel.

So if we get to heaven, it's likely that we will meet people
who weren't visibly Catholic on earth. Nevertheless, however,
those people had a saving connection with the Catholic Church
because they met the conditions explained in *Lumen Gentium*
and were, in the words of *Gaudium et Spes* from the Second Vatican Council, "made partners, in a way known to God, in the
paschal mystery."[7] As to how common this occurs, we simply
don't know. Regardless, you could say that by the time any
person is in heaven, he's Catholic!

The term *saint* can also be applied to non-Catholic Christians on earth who have been validly baptized. Recall from
above that *every* soul united to Christ in baptism is considered
a saint, a "holy one" set apart unto the Lord. So, in this sense, we
can speak of a non-Catholic Christian as a saint.

Concerning whether a pope can canonize a person who
wasn't Catholic during his lifetime, the Church has recognized some such individuals. Various Eastern churches have
come back into full union with the Catholic Church, and
when this happens, the Church honors the saints that these
churches recognized while they were out of full communion.
For example, St. Gregory of Narek was an Armenian who
lived in the tenth century and was not in communion with the
Catholic Church during his lifetime. Despite this, he is recognized as a Catholic saint, and in 2015, he was named a Doctor
of the Church.

There's nothing in principle that prohibits a pope from
doing this. The reason is that the act of canonization is simply
an official declaration that a particular soul is in heaven. And
we've already seen above that it's possible for a non-Catholic to

be saved. Canonizing a non-Catholic would simply be a way of saying that this particular person is one who has met the conditions set forth in *Lumen Gentium.*

Why Canonization?

There's one last question that we need to consider here:"Why do we have official canonizations? What's their purpose?"

Before I give a positive answer, let me first clarify a possible misconception: we do not believe that a canonization gets someone into heaven. This may be evident from what has been said above, but just in case there's any confusion, it's important to get that misconception out the way.

Now, as to a positive answer, the Church canonizes saints primarily to give her children a solid assurance that these individuals are in heaven and thus worthy of our veneration and the invocation of their prayers. As we mentioned in the introduction, we don't want to engage in futile piety.

Also, the Church gives us the saints as examples *par excellence* to imitate in our walk with the Lord. If we strive for the holiness with which they lived their lives, we will attain the reward of eternal life as they did. As for those who lived their lives outside the visible boundaries of the Church and yet are still declared saints, like Gregory of Narek mentioned above, they at least serve as a reminder that we restrain ourselves from making rash judgments concerning the inner movements of a person's heart and mind. We leave such judgments up to God and recognize that he can extend his mercy to whomever he chooses.

Now that we've got straight who and what a saint is, we can start talking about the saints' intercession for us. To this we turn in our next chapter.

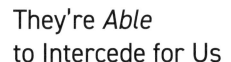

They're *Able* to Intercede for Us

The "*intercession* of the saints" refers to the belief that the blessed in heaven intercede with God on our behalf to obtain benefits from God, whether it be due to God's command or as a response to our requests.

The Council of Trent infallibly taught that the blessed in heaven intercede for us:

> The holy synod enjoins on all bishops, and others who sustain the office and charge of teaching, that, agreeably to the usage of the Catholic and Apostolic Church, received from the primitive times of the Christian religion, and agreeably to the consent of the holy fathers, and to the decrees of sacred councils, they especially instruct the faithful diligently concerning the *intercession* and invocation of saints teaching them, that the saints, who reign together with Christ, *offer up*

their own prayers to God for men. [Those who assert] that *they do not pray for men…* are wholly to be condemned, as the Church has already long since condemned, and now also condemns them.[8]

The *Catechism of the Catholic Church* roots the saints' intercession in their intimate union with Christ in heaven, stating, "Being more closely united to Christ, those who dwell in heaven fix the whole Church more firmly in holiness….They do not cease to intercede with the Father for us….So by their fraternal concern is our weakness greatly helped" (956).

There are two theses that directly pertain to the intercession of the saints: 1) the saints are *able* to intercede for us, both generally and specifically, and 2) the saints in fact *do* intercede for us. The former thesis will be covered in this chapter (chapter two) and the latter in the next (chapter three).

As mentioned in the introduction, before we can even begin asking whether it's appropriate to invoke the saints to pray for us, we need to know whether they're *able* to do so. Do they have knowledge of our affairs here on earth, both general and specific? Would they be able to know the multitudes of specific requests that we make of them, even if they're mental requests and offered by millions, all at the same time?

If it were the case that the saints couldn't intercede, we'd be the most pitiable of Christians, engaging in *futile* piety. There isn't any point in asking the deceased to help us if they can't do it. So it's imperative that we inquire as to whether the saints are *able* to intercede for us.

We answer this question in the positive. Hence our first thesis: the saints are *able* to intercede for us, generally and specifically. Below are arguments both in favor and against the thesis. The favorable arguments don't provide direct proof, but they do give a high degree of *plausibility*. There is a way to biblically *prove* this idea, but we're going to save that evidence for chapter three.

It seems reasonable to start the conversation with the question, "What reason might we have to think that the saints would be able to intercede for us?" And as we'll see, such reasons don't just get the conversation started. They are also interwoven into further discussions in this book, especially in our answers to the arguments against the thesis of this chapter.

Arguments in Favor

From the unfathomable nature of the glorified state in heaven

We can start with the Bible's description of the glorified state in heaven: "What no eye has seen, nor ear heard, nor the heart of man conceived, what God has prepared for those who love him, God has revealed to us through the Spirit" (1 Cor. 2:9-10). St. Paul here describes our heavenly existence as something *very* grand, far beyond what we experience here in this life.

Similarly, St. John recognizes that our status in heaven will be far beyond what we can imagine. We are "God's children," John writes, and in heaven our natures will be elevated to a state that will "be like him," since we will "see him as he is" (1 John 3:2).

Imagine if the saints *couldn't* pray for us. Would our heavenly existence be all that grand? It doesn't seem so! Why would God bestow upon Christians a great dignity to intercede for others while here on earth, a place less grand, and yet revoke such a dignity when they enter heaven, the grandest place of all? The grandeur of glory in heaven, therefore, gives us reason to think the blessed in heaven will be able to pray for us—not just in a general way, but in a specific way, too. Again, it would be a bit underwhelming if we could intercede for specific things only in this life, but not in heaven.

From the supernatural gift of the beatific vision

It's not just the elevated state of our glory in heaven that's significant here. It's also *that which specifically makes* our glory in heaven so grand—namely, the beatific vision. In his 1336 apostolic constitution *Benedictus Deus*, Pope Benedict XII defined this vision as intellectually "seeing the divine essence by intuitive vision…with no mediating creature," where the "divine essence immediately reveal[s] itself plainly, clearly, and openly."[9]

St. John describes this vision: "Beloved, we are God's children now; it does not yet appear what we shall be, but we know that when he appears we shall be like him, for we shall see him as he is" (1 John 3:2). Given that the divine being can't be seen with our physical eyes, John must be referring to an intellectual sight—i.e., knowledge. Paul hints at this knowledge when he writes to the Corinthians, "For now we see in a mirror dimly, but then face to face. Now I know in part; then I shall understand fully, even as I have been fully understood" (1 Cor. 13:12).

To have such a direct knowledge of God's essence, as described above by both Benedict XII and John, requires our finite minds to be elevated by a special grace—what Aquinas called a "created light of glory" (*Summa Theologiae [ST]* I:12:7).[10] We simply don't have by our own power the intellectual "oomph" to get up to that level of knowledge. This is why such a "created light" must be received in the intellect. Since the

Bible reveals that we have such knowledge, the needed grace must be given to the blessed.

Here's where the beatific vision ties into the saints' having the ability to pray for us: if the saints in heaven can receive a grace to know God's essence, then surely it's reasonable to think they'd receive the grace to know our affairs here on earth, the specific requests that we make of them, and the power to intercede for us in response. It's hard to imagine that the saints in heaven would receive such an elevated gift of knowledge in their relationship with God and yet not receive any elevation of knowledge in their relationships with fellow members of the mystical body of Christ.

From the biblical examples of divine infusion of knowledge

The saints' ability to know what's required for them to intercede for us is also biblically plausible when we consider examples of God infusing knowledge into the intellects of human beings. Take the Old Testament story in Daniel 2 involving Daniel and his interpretation of King Nebuchadnezzar's dream.

According to the narrative, Nebuchadnezzar has a troubling dream and asks his sorcerers and wise men to interpret it. But Nebuchadnezzar makes it more difficult by demanding that his wise men first tell him his dream—something the wise men recognize that only the gods could do. "The thing that the king asks is difficult, and none can show it to the king except the gods, whose dwelling is not with flesh" (Dan. 2:11). All of the wise men fail to fulfill the king's request.

We then read in verse 19 that "the mystery was revealed to Daniel in a vision of the night." Afterward, Daniel is able to articulate the dream (and then interpret it) for Nebuchadnezzar.

In other words, God reveals to Daniel the interior thoughts of another man. If God can reveal knowledge of Nebuchadnezzar's dream to Daniel, then he can make known to the saints in heaven the prayer requests that Christians on earth make to them.

From the saints in heaven being perfectly Christlike

In many instances, the Bible speaks of us being transformed to be like Christ. For example, Paul writes in Romans 8:29, "Those whom he foreknew he also predestined to be conformed to the image of his Son, in order that he might be the first-born among many brethren" (see also 1 Cor. 15:49-52, 2 Cor. 3:18, 2 Pet. 1:4). And we know that that transformation will be complete in heaven. We can take another look at 1 John 3:2: "Beloved, we are God's children now; it does not yet appear what we shall be, but we know that when he appears we shall be like him, for we shall see him as he is."

The letter to the Hebrews tells us in 7:25 that Christ, as priest of the heavenly temple, "always lives to make intercession." If Christ always lives to make intercession for Christians on earth, and the saints are going to be perfectly like Christ, it's at least reasonable to think the saints would be doing what Christ does—namely, interceding for Christians on earth. And since Christ's intercession involves knowledge of Christians on earth, even specific knowledge, it's reasonable to infer that such knowledge would be shared with the saints who participate in that intercession.

Arguments Against

The plausibility of the saints' ability to intercede for us will be only as persuasive as our ability to refute the challenges posed to it. If there are definitive reasons to think the saints can't intercede for us, whether those reasons be biblical or theological, then our plausible arguments above are non-starters. So it's necessary that we remove whatever obstacles stand in the way.

We should note that not all of those who oppose Catholics' beliefs about the saints have a problem with the saints' ability to intercede for us. For such folks, *other* things are of more concern—things that we'll cover later in this book. However, there's enough concern among some Christians that justifies an examination of their arguments against the current chapter's thesis.★

The Bible says souls in the afterlife aren't conscious.

Ecclesiastes 9:5 reads, "For the living know that they will die, but the dead know nothing." In verse 10, the author asserts again, "There is no work or thought or knowledge or wisdom in Sheol, to which you are going." If the dead "know nothing,"

★   The major proponents of this challenge come from outside mainstream Protestantism, such as from Seventh-day Adventists like Philip Rodonioff. (See "Waking Up To Eternity," https://www. adventist.org/death-and-resurrection/waking-up-to-eternity.) However, the challenge is also found among non-Seventh-day Adventists.

and there is "no thought or knowledge" in the afterlife, then wouldn't it be futile to ask the saints to pray for us?

Our response to this challenge is that the author is right—at least *generally* speaking. But it doesn't pose a threat to belief in the intercession of the saints. Let me explain.

Before Christ's ascension into heaven, no righteous soul in the afterlife had the beatific vision (see Eph. 4:8). And we don't have any revelation that such souls would have had a habitual grace of infused knowledge besides the beatific vision. Given that such grace would be required for the departed soul to know anything apart from its body (because the natural mode of knowing for the intellect is to use the sensory information received through sensory organs), it follows that the departed souls existing in the afterlife before Christ's ascension would ordinarily not have known anything.[11]

I say *generally* and *ordinarily* because there are examples in the Old Testament of a departed soul engaging in rational activity, and in particular an activity that's ordered to this world. Take 1 Samuel 28:15-19, for example. There Saul consults the "medium at Endor" and requests that she conjure the spirit of Samuel. We're told in verses 15-19 that Samuel communicates with Saul. But how could Samuel communicate with Saul if Samuel were permanently unconscious? Clearly, God gave Samuel's soul at least a *temporary* grace to enable it to know the affairs of Saul despite being in an unnatural state.

We also have the example of 2 Maccabees 15:11-16. Here, Judas Maccabeus has a vision of two men who have died: Onias, the former high priest, and the prophet Jeremiah. Both are engaging in rational activity. Onias is seen "*praying*" for "the entire Jewish nation" (v. 12). Jeremiah is said to offer prayers for Judas and his men as well as for the holy city of Jerusalem. Again, this wasn't the norm, but it's definitely something that happened. If God can give these souls "in Sheol" a temporary grace to know the affairs of men, then it stands to reason that the grace of the beatific vision for the blessed in heaven enables them to do the same.

It not only stands to reason, but it's biblically true. Perhaps the clearest New Testament evidence for consciousness in the afterlife is found in the Book of Revelation. Several times, John describes human souls in heaven in a way that suggests they know what's going on here on earth. Consider, for example, Revelation 5:8:

> And when he had taken the scroll, the four living creatures and the twenty-four elders fell down before the Lamb, each holding a harp, and with golden bowls full of incense, which are the prayers of the saints.

The "twenty-four elders" here are human *souls in heaven*— perhaps deceased leaders of both the Old and New Covenants, which is to say twelve patriarchs and twelve apostles. (It's also speculated that the number twenty-four corresponds to the twenty-four courses of priests who served in the Jerusalem temple.) That they are *human* souls becomes evident in light of the different creatures extending out from the throne of God and the Lamb in concentric circles.[12]

The four living creatures, which are angels, constitute the first circle, as seen in Revelation 4:6. The twenty-four elders make up the second, according to Revelation 4:4. Outside the circle of the twenty-four elders, we're told in Revelation 5:11 that there is a multitude of angels, "numbering myriads of myriads and thousands of thousands." Beyond this large number of angels, Revelation 7:9 tells us there exists "a great multitude which no man could number, from every nation, from all tribes and peoples and tongues, standing before the throne and before the Lamb, clothed in white robes, with palm branches in their hands."

That the multitude is from every nation, tribe, and peoples makes it obvious that it consists of humans and not angels. And since the multitude is identified as "standing before the throne and before the Lamb," we know the people therein are in heaven because the throne of God and the Lamb exists in heaven and not on earth. Moreover, we know that this great multitude consists of human souls in heaven because verse 17 of the same chapter tells us they "shall hunger no more, neither thirst anymore." Then, in verse 19, we read, "God will wipe away every tear from their eyes." To no longer hunger, thirst, or have sorrow is characteristic not of earthly life, but only of the life in heaven.

How can we know that the elders are human souls? Notice the pattern: the four angels, the twenty-four elders, a multitude of angels, and a multitude of human souls. There seems to be a comparison of rank between the two inner groups and the outer two groups. The four angels are higher in rank than the multitude of angels, and the twenty-four elders are higher in rank than the multitude of humans.

If the comparison of rank is angel to angel for the first and third concentric circles, and we know that the fourth circle to which the second group is compared consists of human souls, then it's reasonable to conclude that the second concentric circle of creatures, the twenty-four elders, are human souls. It makes sense that there would be a comparison of rank between two groups of angels and two groups of human souls, with the highest-ranking groups being those closest to God's throne.

Okay, so what are these human souls doing? John tells us they're offering bowls of incense, which the context reveals are the prayers of Christians on earth. How can these elders, human souls, be offering the prayers of Christians on earth if they aren't conscious?

Revelation 6:9-10 is another example. In his vision, John sees under the altar the souls "who had been slain for the word of God," and they cry out, "O Sovereign Lord, holy and true, how long before thou wilt judge and avenge our blood on those who dwell upon the earth?" Notice that the martyrs are fully aware that their enemies are still living on earth. They couldn't know that if they were unconscious.

Another example is Revelation 7:13-14, where an "elder" tells John who the ones "clothed in white robes" are: "These are they who have come out of the great tribulation; they have washed their robes and made them white in the blood of the Lamb." This elder had knowledge that these Christians were martyrs and was aware of the tribulation that they suffered while on earth.

In Revelation 19:1-4, we read about a "great multitude" singing praises to God for judging "the harlot" and avenging "the blood of his servants." When John in Revelation 7:9 introduces this great multitude, standing before the throne and before the Lamb, he specifies that the multitude is "from every nation, from all tribes and peoples and tongues." Therefore, the great multitude John sees singing praises to God consists of (very conscious) human souls.

All the above passages show that human souls in heaven are aware of God's dealings with mankind on earth, friend and foe alike. Ecclesiastes 9:5, 10, therefore, doesn't pose a threat to belief in the intercession of the saints because such a belief pertains to departed souls that *currently* have the beatific vision, a habitual grace of infused knowledge that the departed righteous souls in the Old Testament (before Christ's ascension) didn't have.

> **Given the Church's teaching that a human person *is* a body-soul composite, your prayers can't possibly be directed to St. Peter himself because Peter doesn't exist. Only his *soul* exists.**

This objection arises from the Church's teaching that the human person is a body-soul composite. In 1302, the Council of Vienne authoritatively taught that the soul is the form of the body. It stated,

> With the approval of the above-mentioned sacred council we reprove as erroneous and inimical to the Catholic faith every doctrine or position rashly asserting or turning to doubt that the substance of the rational or intellective soul truly and in itself is not a form of the human body, defining, so that the truth of sincere faith may be known to all, and the approach to all errors may be cut off, lest they steal in upon us, that whoever shall obstinately presume in turn to assert, define, or hold that the rational or intellective soul is not the form of the human body in itself and essentially must be regarded as a heretic.[13]

The implication of this teaching—of the soul being the form of the body—is that the soul and the body are not two distinct natures or substances. Rather, they come together in a human person to form a single nature or substance. The *Catechism* provides an apt commentary:

> The unity of soul and body is so profound that one has to consider the soul to be the "form" of the body [the

Catechism directs the reader to the Council of Vienne here]: i.e., it is because of its spiritual soul that the body made of matter becomes a living, human body; spirit and matter, in man, are not two natures united, but rather their union forms a single nature (365).

Now, this teaching, when applied to a saint at death, seems to be incompatible with the practice of invoking the saints. If St. Peter, as a human person, were the composite of his body and soul, and in death that composite corrupted and went out of existence, it would seem the "human I" of Peter didn't continue to exist. And if that's the case, then it would seem futile to make our requests known to him. Why make a request to someone who doesn't exist (since only his soul exists)?

In 1979, the CDF issued a letter, "On Certain Questions Concerning Eschatology." One question was whether the "human I," or "human self," continues to exist when the soul departs from the body at death. Here is how the CDF responded:

The Church affirms that a spiritual element survives and subsists after death, an element endowed with consciousness and will, so that the "human self" [other translations—"the human I"] subsists. To designate this element, the Church uses the word "soul," the accepted term in the usage of Scripture and Tradition. Although not unaware that this term has various meanings in the Bible, the Church thinks that there is no valid reason for rejecting it; moreover, she considers that the use of some word as a vehicle is absolutely indispensable in order to support the faith of Christians.[14]

To speak of the "human self" or "I" is to speak of what philosophers call the *supposit*. Coming from the Latin word *supponere*, which means "to place under," the *supposit* is the individual subject who *underlies* the acts performed in virtue of the nature that the individual has (see *ST* I:39:1 obj. 3; 29:2; III:2:3). As St. Thomas Aquinas teaches, actions don't belong to the nature or essential principles that constitute the *supposit*, like the rational soul (the substantial form of the human person). Rather, actions belong to the *supposit*, the subject who acts. The subject acts *in virtue of* the essential principles that it has. Here's how Aquinas puts it:

> Action is of a *supposit* according to some nature or form. And therefore actions are not only diversified according to the diversity of *supposits*, but also according to the diversity of nature or form. Just as in one and the same human one action is to see and another is to hear because of diverse powers.[15]

Now, according to the CDF, it's this *supposit,* the individual subject of action, that continues to exist after death. This is what the CDF means in the above quote by "subsist."

How might this be applicable to the saints in heaven? Take Peter, for example. When he walked this earth with our Lord, there was an individual subject of action: Peter. At that time, *he* was the one acting, and he did so (seeing, hearing, and understanding) by way of the principles that made up his essence—his body and soul.

According to the above teaching from the CDF, that same individual subject of action, Peter, continues to exist in heaven. It is *he* (the subject of action) who continues to act when he engages in intercessory prayer. True, *he* (the subject of action) can no longer act by way of the essential principle of his body (he can't see and hear), since *he* (the subject of action) is no longer constituted by his body and his soul together, but rather by his soul alone. But *he* (the subject of action) can act by way of the essential principle of his soul and thereby engage in the rational activity of intercessory prayer.

So we can affirm with the CDF that the individual who is called Peter, the subject of action who walked and talked with our Lord on this earth, *does* continue to exist, albeit he continues to exist in an incomplete state, given that he's constituted by his soul alone. Thus, there's no futility in making our requests known to Peter, because we're not making our requests merely to a soul, as the objection states. Rather, we make our requests known to the same individual *suppositi* who walked with our Lord—that is, Peter.

The Bible says God alone knows the hearts of men.

The practice of invoking the saints' intercession assumes that the blessed can know prayers that we make in our interior thoughts. For many Protestants, both classic and modern, this is a problem because it attributes to the saints a power that the Bible says belongs to God alone.[16]

The second book of Chronicles, in 6:30, reads as follows:

> Then hear thou from heaven thy dwelling place, and forgive, and render to each whose heart thou knowest, according to all his ways (for thou, thou only, knowest the hearts of the children of men).

If the Bible says that only God knows the hearts of men, then the saints can't hear our mental requests for intercession.

Note this challenge targets solely that part of our thesis that says the saints are able to intercede for us in a *specific* way. Some Protestants might be open to the idea that the saints in heaven intercede for us by way of a *general* intercession. This would be akin to what Catholics do in the Mass at the time of the *General* Intercessions: a prayer for world peace, for example, but not for John Smith's heart surgery happening on Wednesday at 4:00 P.M. It's the specificity that gives them a headache.

How do we respond?

There is no reason why God can't reveal his knowledge of our interior thoughts to others. Here is how Aquinas responded to the above challenge in the supplement to his *Summa Theologiae*:

> God alone of himself knows the thoughts of the heart: yet others know them, insofar as these are revealed to them, either by their vision of the Word [the Second Person of the Trinity] or by any other means (*ST Suppl.* 72:1, ad 5).

Notice how Aquinas articulates the difference between how God knows the thoughts of men and how the saints in heaven know the thoughts of men. God alone knows "of himself," whereas the saints know "by their vision of the Word or by any other means."

God knows the interior movements of man's heart and mind by *nature*. In other words, he has this knowledge by virtue of being God. He alone can know the interior thoughts of men in *this way*. But it's not a problem for God to reveal this knowledge to others, such as the saints in heaven, by whatever means he wills.*

We already saw above that God revealed Nebuchadnezzar's interior thoughts and imaginings to Daniel. Peter, in Acts 5:1-5, appears to supernaturally receive knowledge of Ananias's interior thoughts when he chides Ananias for lying to the Holy Spirit by holding back some of the proceeds of his property's sale: "How is it that you have contrived this deed *in your heart*?"

So if God can reveal interior thoughts of others to his saints here on earth, then he can do it for the saints in heaven.

The doctrine of the intercession of the saints makes the saints out to be omniscient.

Some Protestants might counter that for the saints to receive knowledge of the interior thoughts of many people at the same time requires *omniscience*, which only God possesses.[17] But *omniscience*, which is full knowledge of all things (both possible and real—past, present, and future), including the divine essence, isn't the same as knowing a finite number of things at the same time.

So it's not necessary for the saints in heaven to be truly omniscient to know simultaneously the interior prayer requests of Christians on earth. Therefore, it follows that God can communicate this kind of knowledge to rational creatures.

---

* This knowledge is subject to being received in a created intellect because it's not a knowledge that entails full comprehension of the divine essence, which can be had only by God's divine intellect. Our knowledge can't exhaust the divine essence. Only God can fully know himself, as he does in the persons of the Trinity. It requires infinite intellective power to know infinite being.

According to Aquinas, God does this by giving what we spoke of before: a "created light of glory" that is "received into [the] created intellect" (*ST* I:12:7). Because this "created light of glory" is *created*, it's not infinite by nature and doesn't require infinite power to comprehend or act upon. Therefore, it's not impossible for God to give this "created light of glory" to a human or angelic intellect that it may know the interior prayer requests of human beings—even millions of them simultaneously—and respond to them.

The saints must not hear us because they don't save us from harm.

In the supplement to his great work the *Summa Theologiae*, Aquinas poses an interesting objection to the saints' ability to intercede for us (*ST Suppl.* 72:1). It goes something like this: the saints can't possibly be aware of our prayers, because if they were, they would respond to our cries for help amid suffering. Since we still suffer, they must not be aware of our requests. And of course, if they aren't aware of our prayers, then they aren't able to pray for us.

This is not an objection that Protestants use, but they could. And it's interesting to consider.

Behind this question is the idea that a charitable person always assists his suffering friend or neighbor. Since the saints in heaven have perfect love, and we're their friends, it follows that if they know our requests about what's going on in our lives, they will help us in our sufferings.

This objection is based on a false dichotomy. It supposes that either the saints are praying for us, in which case we wouldn't suffer, or they don't know our prayers. But there's a third option.

Perhaps the saints know our prayers, and it's just not God's will that we be delivered from a particular trial, at least not yet. Like us, the saints don't know all of God's plans, so even their petitions are subject to what the Lord wills (see James 4:15).

Alternately, if—in a particular case—they do know that God wills to allow a source of suffering, they certainly would not pray for it to be removed. Aquinas explains:

> The souls of the saints have their will fully conformed to the divine will even as regards the things willed; and consequently, although they retain the love of charity toward their neighbor, they do not succor him otherwise than they see to be in conformity with the disposition of divine justice (*ibid.*).

So if we ask the saints to pray that we be delivered from a particular difficulty in our lives, and it doesn't come to pass, it's because it wasn't God's will. It's not because the saints aren't aware of our prayers.

Furthermore, if God doesn't will to deliver us from a trial, the saints can still help us by praying that we have the strength to persevere in faith and not lose hope amid our suffering. Such prayers also would be fruits of perfect love.

The saints can't know our requests; otherwise, they would know our sufferings and be sad.

There's another objection to the saints' ability to intercede for us that Aquinas considers in the supplement to his *Summa Theologiae* (72:1). It states that the saints don't know our prayers because such knowledge would undermine their happiness.

Here's one way to put the argument:

Premise 1: If the saints knew our prayers, then they would know the sufferings we ask them to help us with.

Premise 2: If the saints knew the sufferings that we ask them to help us with, then the saints would be sad for us.

Premise 3: But the saints in heaven can't be sad.

Conclusion 1: Therefore, the saints can't know the sufferings we ask them to help us with.

Conclusion 2: Therefore, the saints can't know our prayers.

The key premise is the second, to which Aquinas replies that we can't say the saints in heaven are grieved by knowledge of our troubles in life because they are "so filled with heavenly joy, that sorrow finds no place in them" (*ibid.*).

Although I think Aquinas is right here, it seems there needs to be a bit more explanation as to how knowledge of our sufferings wouldn't undermine the happiness of the blessed. A key is found in his *Summa Theologiae*, where Aquinas writes, "God allows evils to happen in order to bring a greater good" (*ST* III:1:3, ad 3).

Whether the saints know that good or not doesn't matter. Simply knowledge *that* God will direct a permitted evil to a greater good gives the saints reason not to be sad. This is especially true given the saints' vision of the divine essence, which provides them with an improved perspective on how God perfectly orders things.

Second, the saints in heaven view the troubles in our lives with an *eternal* perspective, a perspective that Paul articulates in his letters. For example, in Romans 8:18 Paul writes, "I consider that the sufferings of this present time are not worth comparing with the glory that is to be revealed to us." Similarly, in 2 Corinthians 4:17, he writes, "For this slight momentary affliction is preparing for us an eternal weight of glory beyond all comparison."

If Paul's knowledge of this glory without the beatific vision could diminish sadness caused by his sufferings, then how much more would the saints' knowledge of this glory with the beatific vision diminish sadness? Much more!

So, just because the saints in heaven would have knowledge of the troubles in our lives if they knew our prayers, it doesn't follow they would be sad. They know there are greater goods that God is bringing about through our troubles.

CHAPTER 3

They *Do* Intercede for Us

Now that we're on solid ground to think that the saints are *able* to intercede for us, both generally and specifically, the question now becomes, "Is there any evidence that they in fact *do* intercede for us?" This is a reasonable question, because perhaps they are *able* to do so, but God simply wills, in this order of Providence, that they in fact do not. And even if there's no evidence for such a conclusion, without evidence that the saints do in fact intercede, we'd be left merely with plausible arguments, which will be given in this chapter, for their intercession. If we can go beyond mere plausibility, then we ought to.

Along with the thesis in the previous chapter, the thesis that the saints do intercede for us is foundational to the practice of invoking their prayers. So let's look at what sort of arguments we can give to justify this claim.

Arguments in Favor

There are four different kinds of arguments that we can give. The first kind is biblical in nature. These arguments, the first four listed below, range in degrees of persuasive force. One offers only plausibility, whereas the others provide explicit evidence.

The second kind of argument is historical, where we appeal to early Christian sources that testify to an early belief in the intercession of the saints. There are also two arguments below that are theological in nature. One appeals to God's goodness, and the other appeals to the saints' enjoyment of the beatific vision. Although these arguments don't give us certainty via theological demonstrations, they do give strong theological reasons to think the saints do in fact intercede for us.

The fourth kind of argument is an appeal to the miraculous, which goes beyond plausibility and provides certainty. We will look at four miracles attributed to the intercessory prayers of Padre Pio, Fulton J. Sheen, Pope John Paul II, and Mother Teresa.

From the Bible's teaching on the good of mutual intercession among Christians

Given certain things the Bible reveals about Christian intercession, it's reasonable to think the saints in heaven in fact intercede for us.

Consider, for example, St. Paul's practice of and instruction for Christian intercession. Paul tells the Romans in Romans 10:1, "Brethren, my heart's desire and prayer to God for them [my fellow Israelites] is that they may be saved." In 1 Timothy 2:1, Paul urges "that supplications, prayers, intercessions, and thanksgivings be made for all men."

Now, there are good reasons to think that when Paul entered heaven, he didn't stop praying to God that his fellow Jews be saved. The same would be true of other Christians, who would be expected to continue expressing their concern for those on earth by their intercession. Those reasons are as follows.

First, it was charity that moved Paul and other Christians to intercede for one another here on earth in the first place. Well, charity doesn't cease to exist in the soul upon entering heaven. As Paul writes in 1 Corinthians 13:8-12, "Love never ends," unlike prophecies, tongues, and imperfect knowledge, all of which Paul says will pass away when we see God face to face.

Since charity endures in heaven, it's reasonable to conclude that Paul and others, upon entering heaven, would continue to exercise charity and intercede for Christians remaining on earth. (Christians in heaven don't need prayers.)

Second, given that charity endures (and is perfected) in heaven, it's reasonable to think that the saints would not cease heeding Paul's instruction to "bear one another's burdens," which, Paul says, "fulfills the law of Christ" (Gal. 6:2). If the saints in heaven didn't intercede for us, they would no longer help bear our burdens. And if that were true, then they'd no longer be fulfilling the law of Christ.

Perhaps this law of Christ applies only to this life. But that doesn't make sense because it's charity that makes this law binding in the first place, which endures and is perfected for the saints in heaven.

Third, mutual Christian intercession is made possible by virtue of the union all Christians have as members of the mystical body of Christ. Recall, Paul teaches in 1 Corinthians 12:21-26 that each member of the body contributes to the good of the others. Christians in heaven are still members of the mystical body. According to Paul in Romans 8:35 and 39, death can't separate us from that which makes us members of Christ's mystical body: God's love in Christ Jesus.

Therefore, as perfected members of the mystical body of Christ, Christians in heaven, it's reasonable to think, would continue to contribute to the good of other members of the mystical body: us who are here on earth. And a way Christians contribute to the good of others is through intercessory prayer.

Fourth, the saints in heaven are not distracted by the goal of attaining their own salvation, which frees them up to help others attain their salvation. St. Jerome takes this approach in his refutation of Vigilantius, a fourth- and fifth-century priest who opposed several Christian practices of his time, one of which was the invocation of the intercession of the saints. Jerome presents his argument this way: "If apostles and martyrs while still in the body can pray for others, when they ought still to be anxious for themselves, how much more must they do so when once they have won their crowns, overcome, and triumphed?"[18]

From 2 Maccabees 15:11–16

The previous argument showed that it's at least reasonable for a Christian to believe that the saints in heaven intercede for us. We're now going to shift our focus and look at evidence that shows *directly* that they do. The Second Book of Maccabees 15:11–16 is one piece of such evidence. Here's what we read:

> [Judas Maccabeus] armed each of them [his soldiers] not so much with confidence in shields and spears as with the inspiration of brave words, and he cheered them all by relating a dream, a sort of vision, which was worthy of belief.

CH 3: THEY *DO* INTERCEDE FOR US

What he saw was this: Onias, who had been high priest, a noble and good man, of modest bearing and gentle manner, one who spoke fittingly and had been trained from childhood in all that belongs to excellence, was praying with outstretched hands for the whole body of the Jews. Then likewise a man appeared, distinguished by his gray hair and dignity, and of marvelous majesty and authority. And Onias spoke, saying, "This is a man who loves the brethren and prays much for the people and the holy city, Jeremiah, the prophet of God."

Jeremiah stretched out his right hand and gave to Judas a golden sword, and as he gave it he addressed him thus: "Take this holy sword, a gift from God, with which you will strike down your adversaries."

Notice that Judas Maccabeus has a vision of two men who have died: Onias, the former high priest, and the prophet Jeremiah. And both are engaging in intercessory prayer. Onias is seen praying for "the entire Jewish nation." Jeremiah is said to offer prayers for Judas and his men as well the holy city of Jerusalem.

Now, it's true that Protestants don't recognize 2 Maccabees as Scripture. But Catholics do. Therefore, it's legitimate for Catholics to appeal to this passage to inform their religious beliefs concerning God's revelation.

Even for Protestants, this passage has some value in that it attests to the pre-Christian Jewish belief that the faithful departed can intercede on behalf of the faithful here on earth. So the intercession of the saints is not just a Catholic thing.

From Revelation 5:8

Our previous argument looked at explicit biblical evidence from the *Old* Testament. The explicit *New* Testament evidence comes from Revelation 5:8. The text reads,

> When he had taken the scroll, the four living creatures and the twenty-four elders fell down before the Lamb, each holding a harp, and with golden bowls full of incense, which are the prayers of the saints.

The "twenty-four elders" are best understood as human *souls in heaven*, and "prayers of the saints" are best understood as the prayers of Christians *on earth*. Since souls in heaven are seen here as presenting the prayers of Christians on earth to Jesus, Catholics see this text as giving support for the belief that the saints in heaven do in fact pray for us.

But this argument is only as good as the assumptions that it rests upon:

1) that the "twenty-four elders" are human *souls in heaven*,

2) that *saints* in "prayers of the saints" refers to Christians *on earth*, and

3) that *prayers* in "prayers of the saints" refers to *petitions* as opposed to praises.

We already gave reason in the previous chapter to think the "twenty-four elders" are human *souls in heaven*. So let's jump straight to the second assumption: "saints" refers to Christians on earth.

Some Protestants counter that "saints" refers not to Christians on earth, but to those in heaven. Protestant apologist Matt Slick, for example, in his online article "Is Praying to the Saints Biblical?", argues that the term "saints" is a general reference to all the beings surrounding the Lamb's throne—the angels, the creatures, and the elders—who together sing a new song and offer praises to God.[19] Biblical scholar G.K. Beale, in his book *The Book of Revelation*, argues that "saints" refers to the martyrs under the altar in Revelation 6:9-11 who cry out for God to avenge their blood.[20]

To begin, in response, consider that in the New Testament, the term *saint* overwhelmingly refers to human beings on earth, and there are no unambiguous instances where the New Testament uses the term *saint* to refer to a human being in heaven. This gives us reason to be at least *inclined* to think that "saints" in Revelation 5:8 refers to Christians on earth.

Another reason is that the Bible directly associates the prayers of the faithful on earth with incense. For example, the Psalmist writes, "Let my prayer be counted as incense before thee, and the lifting up of my hands as an evening sacrifice!" (Ps. 141:2). If the Bible describes prayers being offered in heaven under the form of incense, and the Bible explicitly associates prayers on earth arising to God with incense, then we have biblical grounds for identifying the prayers of Christians on earth with the "prayers of the saints."

One more point: This image of the elders presenting the "prayers of the saints" to Jesus would have been somewhat familiar to John's Jewish readers, who read the book of Tobit. In Tobit 12:11, the angel Raphael says, "When you and your daughter-in-law Sarah prayed, I brought a reminder of your prayer before the Holy One." Here we have prayers of God's righteous *on earth* brought before the throne of God by an intercessor. In this case, the intercessor is Raphael. In Revelation 5:8, the intercessors are the presbyters. It's not out of bounds to think that John, a Jew who would have been familiar with Tobit, would have interpreted his vision in light of Tobit 12:11, and thereby understood "prayers of the saints" to mean the prayers of God's holy ones *on earth*, like in the case of Tobit and Sarah.

Now, you're probably thinking, "But Protestants don't accept Tobit as inspired." That's true. But Tobit still is a historical source for Jewish belief, and thus, it is acceptable for discerning what a Jew, like John, would have had in mind when he sees the prayers of the saints being presented to Jesus by the elders.

Our appeal to Tobit becomes even more reasonable when we read in Revelation 8:3-4 that the "prayers of the saints," which are mingled with incense, also rise to God from the hand of an angel. Perhaps Raphael?

Now, how do we know that the prayers are *petitions* and not merely *praises* (assumption 3), like the praises that the heavenly inhabitants offer to God and the Lamb in Revelation 5:13 and 7:10?[21] Even if we concede for argument's sake that "prayers" are "praises," it doesn't help to restrict the "saints" to heavenly inhabitants. John tells us in Revelation 5:13 that among those praising God and the Lamb are "every creature in heaven and on earth and under the earth and in the sea, and all therein." If the "prayers" are praises, then the elders are presenting the praises of Christians on earth to God, which would serve as yet another reason to number Christians on earth among the saints in Revelation 5:8.

Moreover, if the twenty-four elders can present the praises of Christians on earth to the throne of God, then it seems reasonable to say that they could present their petitions. There is no good reason to think they couldn't.

Now, there is good reason to think the "prayers" would at least include petitions, if not be restricted to them. Here are some reasons why.

First, although Christians commonly understand prayer to include praise, the common biblical use for the term is as a petition. A look in a biblical concordance reveals as much. Moreover, the Greek word for "prayers" here in Revelation 5:8, *proseuchē*, specifically connotes petitionary prayer rather than praise,[22] for which there are other words (*aineō, epaineō, eulogeō*).[23] The word itself, therefore, *points us to* petitionary prayer.

Second, the elders are depicted as *priests*, which gives us insight to the nature of the prayers being offered. Their status as priests is suggested by the number "twenty-four," which calls to mind the twenty-four divisions of Levitical priests (1 Chron. 24-25) and the offering of incense, which was a priestly duty (Exod. 30:1; Num. 7:84-86, 16:8,10-11).

Inasmuch as they are priests, they "act on behalf of men in relation to God" (Heb. 5:1) in imitation of Jesus, the true priest, "who always lives to make intercession" for those "who draw near to God through him" (7:25). God's people relate to him not just by offering praises. They also relate to him by making petitions: "In everything by prayer and supplication with thanksgiving let your requests be made known to God" (Phil. 4:6).

If the elders in Revelation 5:8 are priests, and their job is to act on behalf of men in relation to God, and God's people relate to God not only by way of praise, but by way of petition, then we can conclude that the prayers of the saints that the elders make present before God involve petitions.

Finally, the motif of prayers being presented before God's throne calls to mind Tobit 12:11 and the description of Raphael presenting the prayers of Tobit and his daughter-in-law to God.

The prayers of both Tobit and Sarah were petitionary (see Tob. 3:1-6,11-15).

As mentioned above, Protestants won't accept this story as inspired. Nevertheless, it does show that the motif of petitionary prayers being presented before God is a part of the Jewish tradition. And given that John the revelator was Jewish, it makes sense that his reference to the prayers of the saints being presented before the throne of God would refer to petitionary prayers.

So let's sum up what we have here: human souls in heaven present prayers of Christians on earth to Jesus. That's intercession! Therefore, Revelation 5:8 gives explicit evidence for the thesis of this chapter: the saints in heaven intercede for us.

From Revelation 6:9-10

Revelation 6:9-10 has already been appealed to as evidence for departed souls engaging in conscious and rational activity. Here, we appeal to it as explicit evidence for their intercessory prayer. The intercession, however, has a bit of a different nature. The text reads as follows:

> When he opened the fifth seal, I saw under the altar the souls of those who had been slain for the word of God and for the witness they had borne; and they cried out with a loud voice, "O Sovereign Lord, holy and true, how long before thou wilt judge and avenge our blood on those who dwell upon the earth?"

It's true that the souls of the martyrs cry out for God's justice here, rather than asking for him to bestow his mercy, which is what we might expect. Nevertheless, they are in fact

interceding, notwithstanding what particularly they're interceding *for*. And if they can do it for God's justice, then they can
do it for God's mercy, too.

Now, someone might counter that this supports only the
notion of the saints' *general* intercession. But it's not much of
a leap to go from general intercession to specific intercession.
The saints can engage in their *general* intercession only by virtue
of the "created light of glory" that we spoke of above. If they
need such a gift to intercede in a general way, then it's no problem for God to give them a similar grace to intercede for us in
a specific way.

From early Christian sources affirming belief in the intercession of the saints

In this argument, we're going to go beyond the boundaries of
the New Testament and look at evidence from early Christian
sources that affirms the intercession of the saints.

The earliest reference outside the New Testament that speaks
of heavenly beings interceding for Christians on earth is the
Shepherd of Hermas, which dates to around A.D. 80. However,
the heavenly being is not a human soul, but an angel. The Shepherd says to Hermas:

> But those who are weak and slothful in prayer hesitate
> to ask anything from the Lord; but the Lord is full of
> compassion, and gives without fail to all who ask him.
> But you, having been strengthened by the holy angel
> [you saw], and *having obtained from him* [the angel] *such
> intercession*, and not being slothful, why do you not ask
> understanding of the Lord, and receive it from him?[24]

It's important that we include this reference because if early Christians believed that angels could intercede for Christians on earth, then it's not a stretch to think they believed that the souls in heaven intercede as well.

St. Clement of Alexandria confirms this line of reasoning at the beginning of the third century (208). He writes in his work *Miscellanies*:

> In this way is he [the true Christian] always pure for prayer. He also prays in the society of angels, as being already of angelic rank, and he is never out of their holy keeping; and though he pray alone, he has *the choir of the saints standing with him* [in prayer].[25]

For Clement, where there's angelic intercession, there's also the intercession of the saints. And such intercessory prayer is conjoined with the prayers of the Christian on earth.

Our next early witness to the intercession of the saints is Origen. In his work *Prayer*, which dates to about 233, he writes:

> But not the high priest [Christ] alone prays for those who pray sincerely, but also the angels...as *also the souls of the saints* who have already fallen asleep.[26]

That Origen speaks of the "saints" as having "already fallen asleep" tells us that he's thinking of the saints in heaven and not Christians on earth. And like Clement, he combines the intercessory prayers of the angels and the saints. For Origen, they go hand in hand.

Our next witness, and perhaps the strongest yet, is St. Cyprian of Carthage. In his *Epistles*, which date to around 252, he writes,

Let us remember one another in concord and unanimity. Let us on both sides always pray for one another. Let us relieve burdens and afflictions by mutual love, that if any one of us, by the swiftness of divine condescension, shall go from here first, our love may continue in the presence of the Lord, and *our prayers for our brothers and sisters not cease* in the presence of the Father's mercy.[27]

Clearly, Cyprian believed that the saints in heaven intercede for Christians on earth.

We could go on providing examples of early Christian sources and beyond that affirm belief in the intercession of the saints. But the above citations suffice for our purposes here.

From God's goodness

We now shift our focus to arguments that are theological in nature. Keep in mind, as mentioned above, these arguments seek to show the *reasonableness* of the thesis that the saints in fact do intercede for us. As such, they're seeking plausibility, not certainty.

One argument is from God's wisdom and goodness, and it's taken from St. Thomas Aquinas in the supplement to his *Summa Theologiae* (72:2). We can start by considering God's goodness and its relation to creatures.

Aquinas starts with a basic truth: God pours out his goodness on things not only by giving things that which is proper to them, like the powers of intellect and will for a human being, but by giving things the power to cause goodness in others. In other words, God works by means of secondary causes. He doesn't just do everything himself directly. He involves creatures and makes them to be real causes of things in the world.

Now, for Aquinas, this is not at all different when it comes to the saints in heaven. Just as God pours out his goodness by making us here on earth real causes of blessings in other people's lives through intercessory prayer, so too it's fitting that God would pour out his goodness by making the saints in heaven real causes of blessings in our lives through their intercessory prayer.

This stands to reason. It doesn't make sense that God would see it fitting to manifest his goodness by making Christians on earth real causes of good in others through intercessory prayer but not the Christians in heaven. What is it about Christians in heaven causing goodness in others that could possibly impede the manifestation of God's goodness? If God saw it fitting to manifest his goodness by making Christians on earth real causes of goodness in others through intercessory prayer, then surely it would be fitting for God to do the same for Christians in heaven.

From the saints in heaven knowing themselves to be co-operators with God in salvation

There's another theological argument that we can give in support of this chapter's thesis. It shows that the saints' factual intercession is reasonable given their experience of the beatific vision. Like the above argument, we turn to Aquinas as our guide.

Again, in the supplement to his *Summa Theologiae*, Aquinas argues that the saints are aware of their role as intercessors and of the requests made of them. He begins with the idea that seeing the divine essence gives knowledge of what pertains to self:

Each of the blessed must needs see in the divine essence as many other things as the perfection of his happiness requires. For the perfection of a man's happiness requires him to have whatever he will, and to will nothing amiss: and each one wills with a right will, to know what concerns himself. Hence since no rectitude is lacking to the saints, they wish to know what concerns themselves, and consequently it follows that they know it in the Word (*ST Suppl.* 72:1).

For Aquinas, the blessed contemplate God in his eternal perfection, seeing in him whatever the perfection of their happiness requires. Aquinas then reasons that such happiness requires that there be nothing lacking in what the blessed will; otherwise, there would be some desire not satisfied, which makes for an incomplete state of happiness.

Next, Aquinas reasons that the will of the blessed in heaven involves knowledge of that which concerns themselves. This is reasonable, given that happiness would be incomplete if there were some further knowledge to be had about the self. The intellect's desire would not be entirely satiated. And Aquinas notes that this is not some egotistical desire to have knowledge of self, since "no rectitude is lacking to the saints," each willing "with a right will."

Therefore, Aquinas concludes, the blessed will to know what concerns themselves, and they see it in God.

The next step of his argument is to show that the saints cooperate with God in assisting the needy in their salvation:

Now it pertains to their glory that they assist the needy for their salvation: for thus they become God's

co-operators, "than which nothing is more Godlike,"
as Dionysius declares (*Coel. Hier.* iii) (*ibid.*).

Aquinas doesn't give a defense of this claim, but the idea
that Christians have a role of cooperating with God in assisting
others to attain their salvation is clearly biblical. Consider, for
example, some of Paul's statements:

- Romans 10:1: "Brethren, my heart's desire and prayer
  to God for them is that they may be saved."

- 1 Corinthians 9:22: "To the weak I became weak, that
  I might win the weak. I have become all things to all
  men, that I might by all means *save* some."

- 1 Timothy 4:16: "Take heed to yourself and to your
  teaching; hold to that, for by so doing you will *save* both
  yourself and your hearers."

Cooperating with God in assisting others to attain their
salvation is clearly part of what it means to be a Christian. And
one way this assistance is carried out, which is pertinent to the
topic at hand, is through intercessory prayer. See Romans 10:1,
again, above.

If assisting fellow Christians to attain salvation through intercessory prayer is essential to what it means to be a Christian on
earth, then surely it would be part of our Christian identity in
heaven. It doesn't make sense that such assistance through intercessory prayer would cease to be part of the Christian life in a
state of existence where the Christian life is perfected.

Remember, the blessed in heaven are those whom God,
in the words of Paul in Romans 8:29, "predestined to be

conformed to the image of his Son." And they are perfectly so. To be perfectly conformed to Christ is to be perfected in what it means to be a Christian. Since being a Christian involves cooperating with God to assist others in attaining their salvation, it follows that it belongs to those in heaven who are perfectly conformed to Christ to be co-operators with God to give such assistance.

Moreover, cooperating with God to assist others to attain salvation through intercessory prayer is a way by which Christians conform themselves to the image of the Son, since the Son, as Hebrews 7:25 describes, "for all time [saves] those who draw near to God through him, since he always lives to make intercession for them." Conformity to Christ involves doing what Christ does.

The blessed in heaven are *perfectly* conformed to Christ. Therefore, it's reasonable to think it still belongs to the blessed in heaven to assist others to attain salvation through intercessory prayer. If they didn't have such a role, then their conformity to the image of Christ would be less perfect in heaven than what it was on earth. But that's absurd!

The last piece of the puzzle for Aquinas is that the blessed must be intellectually aware of that which is necessary to fulfill this role of cooperating with God to assist the needy to attain salvation, which is knowledge of the invocations made of them to assist in salvation. He writes,

> Wherefore it is evident that the saints are cognizant of such things as are required for this purpose; and so it is manifest that they know in the Word the vows, devotions, and prayers of those who have recourse to their assistance (*ibid.*).

51

It would be futile for the saints in heaven to have the role of an intercessor without being able to know the requests made of them.

So far, with Aquinas's help, we have reasons to believe that the saints in heaven have the role of an intercessor and that they would know whatever requests are made of them. But I think we can go a bit beyond what Aquinas says here and ask, how does this imply the idea that the saints *do in fact* intercede for us?

Well, consider that it's God who willed the saints in heaven to play the role as a cooperator with him in helping others attain salvation through intercessory prayer. If that's their God-given role, then it's fitting that God allow them to live out that role and actually intercede. It *doesn't* seem fitting that God would make such a role essential to their Christian identity and never allow them to live it out.

The Angelic Doctor is often most known for his philosophical insights concerning God's existence and nature, the Trinity, and all things pertaining to Christ. But his insights concerning the lower mysteries in the hierarchy of truths are just as profound, and the intercession of the saints is no exception.

From healing miracles attributed to the intercession of the saints

Whenever we're talking about evidence that the saints in heaven intercede for us, it's important that we don't forget the verified miracles attributed to a particular saint's intercession. We're going to look at some of these here.

A Healing Miracle Through St. Pio's Intercession

Let's start with the healing of Consiglia De Martino, attributed to the intercession of St. Pio of Pietrelcina, commonly known as Padre Pio.[28] This particular miracle was used for Padre Pio's beatification.

Martino was a married woman with three children from Salerno, Italy. On October 31, 1995, she had an acute pain in her neck, which eventually became a growth that grew to the size of a grapefruit.

On November 1, she went to Riuniti Hospital in Salerno. She received two CAT scans, both of which revealed that a thoracic duct in her neck had ruptured, diffusing approximately two quarts of lymphatic fluid. It's reported that the doctor affirmed that the surgery would be "difficult and complicated," and it needed to be done "as soon as possible."

Upon receiving the news, Martino turned to the intercession of Padre Pio and called Brother Modestino Fucci at the monastery in San Giovanni Rotondo to inform him of her ailment and request his prayers. Fucci prayed at Pio's tomb.

On November 2, Martino noticed a decrease in the pain in her neck and a rapid diminution of swelling. The doctors examined Martino's decreased swelling the next day, November 3, prior to the scheduled surgery. The x-rays showed not only a complete cure of the rupture of the thoracic duct (the largest vessel of the lymphatic system), which caused the lymphatic spilling, but also the complete disappearance of the large two-quart deposit in her neck, as well as other liquid deposits in her abdomen.

The surgery was canceled and the doctors ordered another CAT scan on November 6, only to find confirmation of the results of the x-ray taken on November 3. Martino was released on November 6. She later underwent more examinations, and none of them showed long-term effects of the condition.

The local diocese conducted its investigation at the Salerno Curia from July 24, 1996 to June 27, 1997, and accepted the validity of the cure with its decree the following September 26.[29] Once the acts of the diocese were published, the documentation was studied by experts and a medical consultant. Unanimously, these experts announced on April 30, 1998 that Martino's cure was "extraordinary and scientifically inexplicable."[30]

The healing was then studied by two special bodies—first by a Special Congress of Theologians on June 22, 1998, and then on October 20 by the Ordinary Session of Cardinals and Bishops.

The crown jewel of this investigation took place on December 21, when, in the presence of Pope John Paul II, the Congregation for the Causes of Saints officially published its decree of Padre Pio's miracle.

A Healing Miracle Through Fulton Sheen's Intercession

The next healing miracle we're going to look at is the healing of baby James Fulton Engstrom, a healing attributed to Ven. Fulton Sheen's intercession. The miracle occurred on September 16, 2010, in Peoria, Illinois. James was delivered stillborn. The umbilical cord had become knotted and cut off blood and oxygen.

When delivered, James didn't have a pulse. His arms and legs were flopped to his sides, and he was blue in color. Being that James was delivered at home, the midwife had to perform CPR on him as they waited for the ambulance. The ambulance came twenty minutes past the delivery and took James to the hospital.

The doctors worked on James with resuscitation techniques and epinephrine injections for about an hour, but to no avail. They decided to declare him dead. Msgr. James Kruse, a diocesan vicar general of the Diocese of Peoria, who participated in the investigation, reports,

> They were continually doing blood tests on the baby, and the one doctor said that the toxicity in his blood was really that of a corpse that was one week or so dead....They were about to declare him dead.[31]

During this time, James's parents were praying to Fulton Sheen, asking for his intercession. At the moment the doctors were about to declare him dead, his heart started beating for the first time, at a rate of 148 beats per minute, normal for a newborn. For a newborn to instantaneously move from life-lessness to ordinary cardiac activity was extraordinary. Kruse reports, "Without any medical explanation, his heart started beating normally, and he was breathing normally, and that's one of the components for a miracle."

What is also extraordinary is that there is no record of someone surviving without a heartbeat and respiration beyond twenty minutes. Jason Gray, Bishop Jenky's appointed episcopal delegate for the inquiry, said, "That's what was known to the medical science and in medical journals."

Given that James was in cardiac arrest and without oxygen for sixty-one minutes, the doctors expected that he would suffer massive organ failure. When there was no organ failure, they predicted severe disabilities, including cerebral palsy, which would require James to be strapped to a wheelchair with feeding tubes for his whole life. They also predicted blindness and virtually no mental activity. James defied the odds and didn't manifest any of these deficiencies or symptoms. He developed like a normal child.

A seven-member panel of medical specialists assembled in Peoria (the place of the miracle) to examine all the medical records associated with the case, as well as James himself.[32] They concluded in March 2014 that James's recovery and development could not be explained through any scientifically known natural causation. Given the circumstances, he should have been either dead or severely disabled.[33] A panel of theologians was subsequently convened and rendered a decision attributing James's restoration to health to a miracle occurring through the intercession of Fulton Sheen.

On July 6, the Vatican Congregation for the Causes of Saints promulgated the decree approving Sheen's miracle.[34]

A Healing Miracle Through Pope John Paul II's Intercession

Next up is the healing of Floribeth Mora Diaz, which was attributed to the intercession of Pope John Paul II. Diaz was a Costa Rican lawyer. She suffered from a brain aneurysm in April 2011. She had a series of tests, including a brain scan, and a three-hour surgery.

The aneurysm didn't leave Diaz on death's bed. Alejandro Vargas, the neurosurgeon who admitted and operated on Diaz, reports there was only a 2-percent chance that another such aneurysm could kill her within a year.[35]

Even with a small chance of another aneurysm causing her death, Diaz began to ask for John Paul II's intercession, including against severe headaches and fatigue.[36] On the night of John Paul II's beatification, Diaz fell asleep, and upon awakening, she heard the voice of John Paul II telling her, "Get up! Don't be afraid!" She got out of bed and told her husband what had happened.[37]

Diaz reports that she immediately felt an "incredible improvement,"[38] no longer feeling fatigued, and felt strong. She believed she had been healed. That July, the relics of Pope John Paul II arrived in Costa Rica, and Diaz, along with her husband, went to see them.

On November 11, Diaz went to the hospital for a resonance test and was scheduled to visit with the doctor the next day to see the results. Here's how she describes that meeting:

> He looked at the monitor and was stunned....He would look at one frame, and then another and another, and continue to be stunned. And when he said that there was nothing wrong, I said, "I knew it."

Vargas describes it from his point of view:

> What we found remarkable, unbelievable really, was that by November there was absolutely no trace in her brain that she ever had an aneurysm....I had never seen this in my career.[39]

Two months later, after detailing on the internet the series of events that led to Diaz's healing, the priest of the parish where she visited the relics was contacted by ecclesiastical authorities from Rome and reached out to Diaz, asking her to undergo some more tests, which she did. The tests all came back as if there had never been anything wrong with her.[40]

She eventually was sent in secret to a hospital in Rome, where they ran more tests and even performed the same surgery on her. Like before, everything showed she was completely healed—there was no trace of an aneurysm.

This healing was eventually confirmed as a miracle by Pope Francis on July 5, 2013 and paved the way for John Paul II's canonization the following April.

A Healing Miracle Through Mother Teresa's Intercession

It's appropriate to follow a miracle attributed to the intercession of Pope John Paul II with a miracle that occurred through the intercession of Mother Teresa, given that they were good friends and all. The miracle is that of Monica Besra in Bengali, India.

In 1998, Monica had swelling in her abdomen caused by accumulation of fluid in the tissues—called *tumefaction*—that measured to about 6 inches.[41] It was unclear as to whether the growth was due to cancer or tuberculosis.[42]

The growth caused great pain for Monica, which she describes as follows: "For two months I had severe pain, terrible pain, and I was crying. I was not able to sleep; I could lie only on the left side and I couldn't stand straight."[43]

In another interview, Monica further describes her condition:

> I was so ill I couldn't eat anything. I would immediately throw up. The Sisters of Missionaries of Charity even took me to a doctor in Siliguri, but he said I might not regain consciousness if operated upon.[44]

Monica reports that her sister eventually took her to the newly opened Missionaries of Charity center near their village the day before the first anniversary of Mother Teresa's death, September 4. Their purpose was to ask the sisters for prayers. Monica details her visit:

> I was too ill to move, but two sisters supported me there. There was a photograph of Mother Teresa there. When I entered the Church a blinding light emanated from Mother's photo and enveloped me.

I didn't know what was happening. I was too ill to sit
for long and was soon brought back to my bed.

It's reported that the sisters put a medal of Mary that had
been touched to Mother Teresa's body over Besra's abdomen
and asked for Mother's intercession.[45] Upon waking the next
day (eight hours later), Monica found that her stomach was
much smaller, and the lump disappeared three days later.[46] And
to what did she attribute this? Monica confidently asserts, "I
am sure that Mother Teresa made me all right."

After this, the sisters took Monica to a doctor to get checked
out. The medical exams showed that the abdominal mass was
gone and that she no longer needed surgery.[47] The occurrence
was reported to the local diocese, and a team of diocesan investigators interviewed Monica and a series of doctors, all of whom
confirmed that the abdominal mass had disappeared. (Nine of
the eleven were not Catholic.) With the information provided
by the investigators, the archbishop of Calcutta, Henry D'Souza,
declared, "The Probe found the miracle to have met the essential requisites of being organic, immediate, permanent and
intercessionary in nature."[48] The miracle was recognized by the
Vatican in 2002 and was used for Mother Teresa's beatification.

Now, although doctors did not doubt the disappearance of
the mass, a few of them decried the *miraculous explanation*, attributing the disappearance to science. Mainul Islam, one of the
local doctors, denied the story altogether: "It isn't possible for
someone with a tumor to be cured like that."[49] Another doctor,
Ranjan Kumar Mustafi, said in an interview with the station
NDTV, "We treated Monica Besra for her illness. There was
no such thing as a miracle. Medical science cured her."[50] Some
doctors took the route and claimed that it wasn't a tumor, but a
cyst, from which Monica recovered after prolonged treatment.[51]

But the statements by the above doctors shouldn't cast doubt on the miraculous nature of the event. Why? Doctors had been treating Monica with no success. Monica says as much: "I visited many doctors, underwent a long medication process, but nothing helped."[52] These doctors can't attribute the disappearance of the mass to their treatments when their treatments failed time and time again. For the mass to go away *only after* the sisters invoked Mother Teresa's intercession gives us good reason to think that medicine is not the deciding factor here.

Arguments Against

The arguments against the thesis that the saints in fact intercede for us are of two types: biblical and theological. The biblical argument targets our above comments on Revelation 5:8. The two theological arguments derive from the Church's teaching on the saints' inability to merit in heaven and on the perfect conformity of their wills to God's will.

> **Revelation 5:8 shows that the twenty-four elders intercede only in a *general* way. It doesn't get you to the Catholic position of the saints knowing our hearts and minds.**

Some Protestants[53] are okay with conceding that Revelation 5:8 reveals the saints in heaven intercede for us, but only in a *general* way. They don't think this text gives the Catholic what he's after, since it doesn't indicate that the elders "hear" (have knowledge of) the specific requests made to them, assuming that the prayers were even requests. It says only that the elders present Christians' prayers in the form of incense. Again, that seems to be merely an affirmation of *general* intercession, not intercessory prayers for specific requests.

It's true that the text doesn't *explicitly* state that the elders "hear" the prayers and thereby indicate that they know the specific requests made to them. But I do think there are reasons to believe that the elders "hear" (have knowledge of) the specific prayers.

For starters, the text specifies that the elders are presenting the "prayers of the saints." It doesn't say they were simply interceding for Christians on earth. If these were merely *general* intercessory prayers, it wouldn't be necessary to include the "prayers of the saints" as part of the equation.

Now, it's this part of the equation, the offering of the "prayers of the saints," that leads us to further reasons why these elders would have knowledge of specific requests made to them. Consider that the incense is simply a symbol for the prayers, which by nature are *immaterial*. More particularly, they're immaterial *ideas*. It's not as if the contents of the prayers were enclosed within an envelope that the elders lay hold of and carry to the Lamb as heavenly mailmen. Since the prayers can be only immaterial ideas, the only way that the elders could possibly present the prayers to Jesus would be to *know* them.

What's more, as we noted above, the elders are *priests*. Jewish priests knew the contents of the prayers that Jews offered to the Lord when they interceded for them, whether it was the particular sin that a sin offering was offered for (Lev. 5:5-6; see also Lev. 6) or the thanksgiving given to God with the peace offering (Lev. 7:11-13). Given that the elders are exercising an active *priestly* role in heaven, as mentioned above, it's reasonable to think they would know the contents of the prayers.

Finally, recall from Tobit 12 that Raphael "brought a reminder of [Tobit's and Sarah's] prayer before the Holy One"

THE SAINTS PRAY FOR YOU

(v. 11). Raphael seems to *know* the contents of the prayers of Tobit and his daughter-in-law. Both Tobit's and Sarah's petitionary prayers are recorded in Tobit 3:1-6 and 11-15.

Perhaps it could be that Raphael tells God, "Hey, God, remember that Tobit and Sarah *said a prayer*." But this doesn't seem to fit the *precise knowledge* that Raphael has of the earthly affairs of Tobit and Sarah: he knows that they "buried the dead" (v. 12), he knows that they "did not hesitate to rise and leave" dinner "in order to go out and lay out the dead" (v. 13), and he knows the physical ailments that both Tobit and Sarah suffered—"now God sent me to heal you and your daughter-in-law Sarah" (v. 14). To say that Raphael didn't know the contents of the prayers is a bit out of place.

Given that we can read Revelation 5:8 in light of Tobit 12:11-15, as discussed above, it's reasonable to think that the elders in Revelation 5:8 know the contents of the prayers offered, just as Raphael seemingly knows the contents of the prayers offered by Tobit and Sarah.

So Revelation 5:8 in fact does get a Catholic what he's looking for in terms of biblical support for the saints' *specific* intercession. You just have to think through the text a bit and unpack it.

The saints can't merit anymore anyway.

Now that we've considered a biblical argument against the saints in fact interceding for us, let's consider some arguments that are theological in nature, both of which come from St. Thomas Aquinas.

We can't really improve on his formulation of this first argument, so here it is:

> Whosoever obtains something by prayer merits it in a sense. But the saints in heaven are not in the state of meriting. Therefore they cannot obtain anything for us from God by their prayers (*ST Suppl.* 72:2, obj.4).

The standard view in Catholic theology is that in order for a person to merit something, he must still be in this life, so departed human souls—including the saints—can no longer merit. Here are some biblical passages that theologians have traditionally appealed to for support of this teaching:

- Hebrews 4:10: "For whoever enters God's rest also ceases from his labors as God did from his."

- Revelation 14:13: "Blessed are the dead who die in the Lord henceforth. 'Blessed indeed,' says the Spirit, 'that they may rest from their labors, for their deeds follow them!'"

Now, St. Paul teaches in 1 Corinthians 3:8 that the wages we receive are proportioned to our labor. He writes, "He who plants and he who waters are equal, and each shall receive his wages according to his labor."

So, if the Bible teaches that our labors cease when we die in the Lord, and our wages are proportioned to our labors, then it follows that our wages for our labors are fixed upon death. And since "wages" here traditionally has been viewed to include the gift of charity, we can conclude that our degree of charity is fixed upon death, and thus we can no longer merit because charity is the principle of merit.[*]

There are a few different possible answers to this objection that Aquinas identifies.

First, as he writes, "although the saints are not in a state to merit for themselves, when once they are in heaven, they are in a state to merit for others." In other words, rather than their charity benefiting themselves, it's beneficial for others.

A second possibility is that the saints in heaven can assist others by virtue of the merit they acquired while here on earth. Aquinas writes, "For while living they merited that their prayers should be heard after their death."

The *Catechism* adopts Aquinas's answer here in its teaching on the intercession of the saints, making the merits that the saints carry with them into heaven an integral part of the doctrine. Paragraph 956, quoting *Lumen Gentium* 50, reads as follows:

> *The intercession of the saints.* "Being more closely united to Christ, those who dwell in heaven fix the whole Church more firmly in holiness.... They do not cease to intercede with the Father for us, *as they proffer the merits* [hold out to someone for acceptance] *which they acquired on earth* through the one mediator between

---

[*] Some theologians throughout the history of the Church have argued that perhaps the soul can increase in charity while in purgatory—not because of new movements of love while in purgatory, but rather because of the past merits acquired in life. On this view, the increase of charity in purgatory would be more of an unfolding of their earthly merits. See Robert Bellarmine, *On Purgatory: The Members of the Church Suffering*, trans. Ryan Grant (Post Falls, ID: Mediatrix press, 2017), 154-155.

God and men, Christ Jesus....So by their fraternal concern is our weakness greatly helped."

Of course, the above teaching presupposes the entire notion of the treasury of the Church. In paragraphs 1475-1477, the *Catechism* explains the Church's treasury as follows:

In the communion of saints, "a perennial link of charity exists between the faithful who have already reached their heavenly home, those who are expiating their sins in purgatory and those who are still pilgrims on earth. Between them there is, too, an abundant exchange of all good things." In this wonderful exchange, the holiness of one profits others, well beyond the harm that the sin of one could cause others....

We also call these spiritual goods of the communion of saints the Church's treasury....The "treasury of the Church" is the infinite value, which can never be exhausted, which Christ's merits have before God.... This treasury includes as well the prayers and good works of the Blessed Virgin Mary....In the treasury, too, are the prayers and good works of all the saints.

Now, lest someone think this teaching on the Church's treasury is unbiblical, it's right in line with what the Bible says about how the value of our charitable works remains with us as we enter heaven. For example, as we saw just above, St. John writes in Revelation 14:13, "I heard a voice from heaven saying, 'Write this: Blessed are the dead who die in the Lord henceforth.' 'Blessed indeed,' says the Spirit, 'that they may rest from their labors, for their deeds follow them!'" The value of the good works of those who die in grace continues to exist as they exist in heaven.

So what both Aquinas and the *Catechism* are saying is that the saints in heaven intercede for us by directing to the good of others (Christians on earth) the value (the merit) of the good works they performed on earth. This being the case, the saints' inability to merit in heaven poses no threat to the thesis of this chapter. Their intercessory prayer could be by virtue of the merit already attained through the love they exercised while on earth.

A third possible response is that the objection assumes that prayer obtains things only by way of merit. But, Aquinas argues, this is not true. Prayer can also obtain things by way of *impetration*, which simply means "by request or entreaty."

Prayer is meritorious when there is a certain proportion between our prayer and that which we seek to obtain through the prayer, such that the thing we seek through the prayer is given as a reward. For example, Paul teaches in Romans 2:6-7 that eternal life will be given to those "who by patience in well-doing seek for glory and honor and immortality." The reason why eternal life is a proportionate reward for our good works is that, according to Philippians 2:13, it is God who is at work in us, "both to will and to work for his good pleasure." Or, as Paul puts it in Galatians 2:20, "it is no longer I who live, but Christ who lives in me." The supernatural reward of heaven has a proper proportion to the supernatural value that God gives our good works by acting in and through us.

Obtaining something through prayer considered merely as a request (impetration), on the other hand, depends not on a proportion between the value of the request and that which is sought, but rather on the liberality of the person from whom we're requesting something. In other words, whatever is sought by the request is not in any way due to the person who's making the request. Whether the thing sought is obtained is entirely up to the person of whom the request is made.

So we can conclude with Aquinas that although the saints in heaven might not be able to obtain some good for us through meritorious prayer, they can still obtain that good through prayers of impetration—prayers by way of request or entreaty.

The saints only will what God wills.

Aquinas considers another objection that could be made against the belief that the saints intercede for us (*ST Suppl.* 72:3, ad 5). It's based on the conformity of the saints' wills to God's will, and it has a number of steps that can be put this way:

Step 1: The saints conform their wills perfectly to the will of God.

Therefore, the saints only will what they know God to will.

Step 2: The saints' intercessory prayers necessarily involve what the saints will.

Therefore, the saints' intercessory prayers necessarily involve praying only for what they know God to will.

Step 3: Whatever God wills can still be done without the saints having prayed for it.

Therefore, the saints' prayers are not efficacious for obtaining anything.

Aquinas accepts every step of the argument—except where it jumps to the conclusion in step three. That God can bring about any effect without the saints praying for it doesn't mean that saints' prayers can't be a (secondary) cause of some effects.

His reason is that God wills that the prayers of the saints be the means by which he brings about an effect. In other words, God wills the saints' prayers to be secondary causes of goodness in our lives.

This harkens back to what we said before. God manifests his goodness by bestowing upon his creatures the power to be real causes of good in others, including our prayers of intercession as well as those of the saints. To put it simply, God may will that some blessing not be given except through a saint's intercessory prayer.

This is what we mean when we speak of a prayer "causing" something. It does not mean that the prayer has any power in and of itself. If I ask you to pray for me to be healed and God chooses to grant your prayer request, the ultimate cause of the effect was God—not some magic words you said. But, in another sense, I could say that your prayer "caused" my healing in a looser sense—in that it was the thing God chose to act on.

The same applies to the saints in heaven. The saints do not have magical powers. But we can speak of their prayers being "causes" in this loose sense—when God chooses to act on them—though the real power always belongs to God.

We can shed further light on Aquinas's argument by understanding that God's providence involves willing not only certain effects to take place, but also the causes from which those effects will be brought about. That is to say, God wills a pattern of cause-effect relationships.

Now, the eternal decree that determines which causes will bring about which effects includes human acts. These actions are an essential part of God's plan. In the words of Aquinas, they "achieve certain effects according to the order of the divine disposition" (*ST* II–II:83:2).

Consider an example. God decreed from all eternity that I would have a fried egg for breakfast this morning. This eternal decree involved the egg being produced in a way that involved my wife's act of love to cook it for me (she's so sweet), along with all the other ways in which a fried egg comes about: the egg is cracked, put into the frying pan, and cooked by the heat inhering in the frying pan caused by the fire on the gas stove. My wife's actions, along with all the other natural processes of cooking an egg, were willed by God to be a part of the cause-effect pattern.

The same is true with intercessory prayer, whether we're talking about the prayers of Christians on earth or in heaven. Intercessory prayer is simply one human action among many (like my wife cooking the egg) that God wills to be a cause of certain effects in his divine plan.

Intercessory prayer requests from God that which he has willed from eternity to be bestowed by that intercession. As philosopher Brian Davies explains, "God may will from eternity that things should come about as things prayed for by us"—or, for our purposes, prayed for by the saints.[54]

In other words, it's possible that God wills some events to occur only as a result of the saints' intercession. For example, God may have eternally decreed to heal the cancer of a loved one, but only on condition that persistent requests for a miracle be made through the intercession of a particular saint.

Whether we know that the effect is conditioned by the request or not doesn't matter. The point is, it's possible, so we make the request hoping that God wills the saints' intercession to be a cause of the effect. If it turns out that he did not will it, then we trust that God has good reasons for his choice. This is why Christians pray, "Thy will be done."

But if God wills a saint's intercession to be the cause of the desired effect, then it would be true to say the saint's prayer made a real difference. It would make a difference by being an essential part of the cause-effect pattern God has eternally decreed.

The real causal power that the saints' prayers have in God's eternal plan is not at all different from the real causal power my wife's actions have in producing a fried egg when she cooks breakfast for me. Her actions are essential for the fried egg, because that is how God from all eternity arranged it to be. God has created a world in which fried eggs come to be in a specific way.

Similarly, with regard to the saints' intercession, some events will occur only as a result of their intercessory prayer, because that is the specific way God has arranged it. God has created a world in such a way that our actions, including prayer, serve as game-changers in the history of the world.

The bottom line is this: there is nothing in the saints' conformity to the divine will that makes it incompatible with the saints' intercessory prayer being effective in our lives. Their petitions are arranged by God to be part and parcel of his divine plan—a great honor God bestows upon them as real causes of good in others.

CHAPTER 4

It's Good to Invoke Them

The "*invocation* of the saints" refers to the practice of requesting that the saints in heaven intercede for us. The Council
of Trent's infallible teaching on the good of invoking the saints
is tied to its teaching on the intercession of the saints, which
we sourced in the quote at the beginning of chapter two. Here
it is again, but with an emphasis on the parts that pertain to the
invocation of the saints.

> The holy synod enjoins on all bishops, and others
> who sustain the office and charge of teaching, that,
> agreeably to the usage of the Catholic and Apos-
> tolic Church, received from the primitive times of
> the Christian religion, and agreeably to the consent
> of the holy Fathers, and to the decrees of sacred

councils, they especially instruct the faithful diligently concerning the intercession and *invocation* of saints… that *it is good and useful suppliantly to invoke them*, and *to have recourse to their prayers, aid, (and) help* for obtaining benefits from God, through his Son, Jesus Christ our Lord, who alone is our Redeemer and Savior; but that they think impiously…who deny that the saints, who enjoy eternal happiness in heaven, are to be *invocated*…or, that *the invocation of them to pray for each of us* even in particular, is idolatry; or, that it is repugnant to the word of God; and is opposed to the honor of the one mediator of God and men, Christ Jesus; or, that it is foolish to supplicate, vocally, or mentally, those who reign in heaven…are wholly to be condemned, as the Church has already long since condemned, and now also condemns them.[55]

As we pointed out in the introduction, some Christians may be willing to accept that the saints intercede for us. But they refuse to make the move from affirming the saints' intercession to invoking their prayers. There are several reasons for this, as we'll see below. But first, let's consider some arguments in *favor* of the practice, and thereby establish the "good" and usefulness of invoking of the saints' intercessory prayers.

Arguments in Favor

Like before, the arguments that we will examine here vary in kind. The first four appeal to *biblical* principles from which we can infer the good of invoking the saints' intercession. Christians who assent to the 1646 Westminster Confession should have no problem with such inferences, since that document states that "the whole counsel of God concerning all things necessary for his own glory, man's salvation, faith and life, is either expressly set down in Scripture, *or by good and necessary consequence may be deduced* from Scripture."[56]

The last two arguments in favor of invoking the saints are theological and historical in nature. The theological argument appeals to God's wisdom, and the historical appeals to the early Christian witnesses of the practice of invoking the saints. We begin with the biblical arguments.

From invoking other Christians' intercessory prayers

The Bible is clear that it is good for Christians to invoke the intercession of other Christians for obtaining benefits from God. Consider, for example, St. Paul's request that the Romans intercede for him:

> I appeal to you, brethren, by our Lord Jesus Christ and by the love of the Spirit, to strive together with me in your prayers to God on my behalf, that I may be delivered from the unbelievers in Judea, and that my service for Jerusalem may be acceptable to the saints, so that by God's will I may come to you with joy and be refreshed in your company (Rom. 15:30-32).

Paul explicitly requests that the Christians in Rome pray "to God on [his] behalf." And he prays that he may attain benefits: 1) to be delivered from his enemies and 2) that his ministry be accepted by Christians. So the Bible approves of one Christian invoking another Christian to pray to God on his behalf to attain certain benefits.

Now, the saints in heaven are Christians. In fact, they're the most perfect Christians because they are perfected in charity and have the beatific vision. Recall what we said above: the saints in heaven have not ceased being members of the mystical body of Christ. As Paul teaches in Romans 8:35 and 39, death can't separate us from that which makes us members of Christ's mystical body: God's love in Christ Jesus. This being the case, our invocation of their intercessory prayers fits Paul's invocation of the intercessory prayers of the Christians in Rome: one Christian invoking the intercessory prayers of other Christians. According to the Bible, that's a good and useful thing to do. The only difference is that for Paul, the Christians he invokes are in Rome, and for us, the Christians we invoke are in heaven.

Perhaps this difference is significant for some. We already looked in chapter two (doubts concerning whether the saints would be *able* to intercede for us) at some possible reasons why this would be a problem. Other possible reasons will be addressed below. But at least the problem would not be the act of *invocation* itself. Rather, it would be *whom* we're invoking.

From James 5:16

Our invocation of the saints' intercession also fits within God's divine order expressed by St. James in James 5:16: "The prayer of a righteous man has great power in its effects." We mentioned above that the saints in heaven are perfected members of the mystical body of Christ. As Hebrews 12:23 puts it, they are "the spirits of just men made perfect."

Now, what are they perfected in? Righteousness! They are *perfectly* ordered to God as their supernatural end.

Therefore, our invocation of the saints' intercessory prayers is our request for the prayers of "a righteous man." And if it's good and useful to request the prayer of a righteous man, which James makes clear—it "has great power in its effects"—then it's good and useful to request the prayers of the saints in heaven.

From 1 Corinthians 12:20-21

Several times already in this book we've had the opportunity to appeal to Paul's teaching on the mystical body of Christ and our membership in it as Christians. Here we have yet another opportunity.

Chapter 12 of Paul's first letter to the Corinthians is the locus of his teaching on the mystical body of Christ. In verse 13, he reveals what's required for entrance into this body: "For by one Spirit we were all *baptized* into one body." In the subsequent verses, Paul compares the members of this mystical body to different members in a physical body: an eye, a hand, a head, feet, etc. (vv. 14-21). He then reflects on how each of those members within a body assists other members by performing different functions in the body (vv. 22-26). It's within this context that Paul gives his teaching in verses 20-21:

> As it is, there are many parts, yet one body. The eye cannot say to the hand, "I have no need of you," nor again the head to the feet, "I have no need of you."

For Paul, each of these members of a physical body represents Christians as members of the mystical body of Christ. Therefore, Paul is forbidding us as Christians to deny the help of other Christians. We can't say to another Christian, "I have no need of you."

Now, to say the invocation of the saints' intercessory prayers is inappropriate is tantamount to saying that it is inappropriate to request the help of another Christian. But wouldn't that violate Paul's teaching? Wouldn't that be akin to one member of the body of Christ saying to another, "I have no need of you"? It would! Lest we're willing to go against Paul here, we must acknowledge that it is good and useful to invoke the saints to intercede for us.

From Acts 9:36-41

St. Peter's actions in Acts 9:36-41 provide us a principle that can govern our reflection on the appropriateness of invoking the saints.[57] St. Luke recounts the story of Peter raising from the dead a female Christian disciple from Joppa. He makes clear in verse 4 that she was dead , stating, "In those days she fell sick and *died.*"

Upon hearing that Peter was near, some disciples sent for him. He came to where Tabitha's dead body lay, "knelt down," and "prayed" (v. 40). Luke tells us Peter then turned to the body and said, "Tabitha, rise."

Now, you might be thinking, "What in the world does this have to do with the invocation of the saints?" Well, although Peter doesn't technically invoke a deceased Christian—that's to say, he doesn't ask her for help—he does issue a *command* to her, which is an invocation of sorts. And if it's appropriate for Peter to issue a *command* to a deceased Christian, then it stands to reason that it would be appropriate for him (and us) to issue a *request.*

From early Christian sources affirming belief in the invocation of the saints

In the last chapter, we looked at historical sources within early Christianity that attested to belief in the *intercession* of the saints. Here, we're going to look at some sources that attest to the practice of *invoking* the saints.

The earliest evidence we have is an early to mid-third-century hymn that was prayed by Christians in Egypt, called *Sub Tuum Praesidium*. It's generally dated to around 230-250. The hymn is found on a scrap of papyrus called *Rylands Papyrus* 470.[58]

Here's the money quote:

> Beneath your compassion, we take refuge, O Theotokos: do not despise our petitions in time of trouble: but rescue us from dangers, only pure, only blessed one.

Next up are early Christian inscriptions. Consider, for example, a grave inscription that speaks of someone named Gentianus:

> Gentianus, a believer, in peace, who lived twenty-one years, eight months, and sixteen days, and *in your prayers ask for us*, because we know that you are in Christ.[59]

The mid-third century doesn't just have inscriptions on graves. The catacombs also have many inscriptions that invoke the saints for their intercession. Take, for example, the so-called *Memoria Apostolorum*, a series of inscriptions in the funerary area of St. Sebastian on the Appian Way that invoke Ss. Peter and Paul for their intercession. One, dating to 250, reads, "Peter and Paul,

remember us."[60] Many believe that this gives evidence that the
relics of Peter and Paul were transported on the Appian Way
during the years of Valerian's persecution.

At the beginning of the fourth century, we have further
evidence that Christians made requests from the Blessed Virgin
Mary. Consider Methodius of Philippi, for example:

> We pray you, the most excellent among women, who
> boastest in the confidence of your maternal honors
> that you would unceasingly keep us in remembrance.
> O holy Mother of God, remember us, I say, who make
> our boast in you, and who in august hymns cele-
> brate the memory, which will ever live, and never
> fade away.[61]

The request that Mary "remember" them is not merely a request
for mental remembrance, but a request for intercessory prayer.

In St. Cyril of Jerusalem's *Catechetical Lectures*, which dates
to around 350, we discover that the intercession of the saints
was invoked in the liturgy. Speaking of the Eucharistic Prayer,
Cyril writes,

> We commemorate also those who have fallen asleep
> before us, first patriarchs, prophets, apostles, martyrs,
> that at their prayers and intercessions God would
> receive our petition.[62]

Ephraim the Syrian, in his *Commentary on Mark* (c. 370),
makes several requests of the martyrs in heaven, whom he calls
"saints." He writes,

> You victorious martyrs who endured torments gladly for the sake of the God and Savior, you who have boldness of speech toward the Lord himself, you saints, intercede for us who are timid and sinful men, full of sloth, that the grace of Christ may come upon us, and enlighten the hearts of all of us so that we may love him.[63]

In St. Gregory of Nazianzen's *Orations* (374), we find the principle that the saints' intercession in heaven is more effective than it was here on earth. Speaking of his father's intercession, he writes,

> Yes, I am well assured that [his] intercession is of more avail now than was his instruction in former days, since he is closer to God, now that he has shaken off his bodily fetters, and freed his mind from the clay that obscured it, and holds conversation naked with the nakedness of the prime and purest mind.[64]

The last early Christian source we'll reference here is St. John Chrysostom. In his *Homilies on Second Corinthians* (392), he writes,

> He that wears the purple himself goes to embrace those tombs, and, laying aside his pride, stands begging the saints to be his advocates with God, and he that has the diadem implores the tent-maker and the fisherman, though dead, to be his patrons.[65]

To beg the saints to advocate with God on our behalf is to request their intercessory prayer.

In light of this evidence, we can conclude that the belief that the saints intercede for us and our invoking their prayers are not something the Church made up late in its history. Rather, it was part of historic Christianity.

From God's wisdom

In the previous chapter, we gave a theological argument from God's *goodness* for the thesis that the saints in fact do intercede for us. A similar argument from God's *wisdom* can be given for the thesis of this chapter: it's appropriate for Christians to invoke the intercessory prayers of the saints. Like the previous argument, we derive *this* argument from St. Thomas Aquinas (*ST Suppl.* 72:2).

The basic principle that Aquinas begins with here is that God has established an order among things whereby the last should be led to God by those that are midway between. This maps nicely with our Christian experience.

For example, when we first encounter the Lord and enter a relationship with him, we often seek the counsel of those who are holier than we are to gain insight as to how to progress in our relationship with Jesus. Whenever we need prayer, we tend to ask those who we know are farther along on the path of holiness, since we know James's teaching in James 5:16 that the prayer of a righteous man avails much.

We even follow this order in our everyday lives, when God is not necessarily the explicit goal we're trying to achieve. For example, whenever we want to gain knowledge and learn about a topic, we go to someone who has more knowledge than we do. Theoretically, God could just infuse the knowledge in our minds. But that's not how he set it up.

Given this divine order of the last being led to God by those who are midway, Aquinas concludes that we should be led to God through the intercession of the saints. He writes,

> Since the saints who are in heaven are nearest to God, the order of the divine law requires that we, who while we remain in the body are pilgrims from the Lord, should be brought back to God by the saints who are between us and him: and this happens when the divine goodness pours forth its effect into us through them (*ibid.*).

How does this apply to our invocation of the saints? Well, our invocation of their prayers *fits* this divine order. We, who are farther away from God, request that they, who are closer to God, aid us in our journey back to God. And any Christian practice that fits within God's divine order is an appropriate Christian practice.

Arguments Against

The Catholic practice of asking the saints to pray for us contradicts 1 Timothy 2:5.

A common objection that some Protestants make to the Catholic practice of requesting the saints' intercession is that it contradicts 1 Timothy 2:5, where Paul writes, "There is one mediatory between God and men, the man Christ Jesus."[66] If Christ is the one mediator, so it goes, then asking for the saints' intercession would seem to imply that Christ's mediation is not good enough.

How should we respond?

First, the objection assumes that to ask the saints to pray for us takes away from Christ's unique mediation. But this line of reasoning contradicts Christian teaching and practice because it belongs to the Christian life to ask for the intercession of other Christians. If we were to follow the logic embedded in this challenge, then we would have to deny all forms of Christian intercession, which, from a Christian point of view, is absurd.

Even the context of the passage in question proves that intercessory prayer is essential to Christian life. In verse 1, Paul encourages Christian intercession: "I urge that supplications, prayers, intercessions, and thanksgivings be made for all men." Then, in verse 4, he says such prayers and intercessions are "acceptable in the sight of God our Savior." Other such passages include Romans 15:30; 2 Corinthians 1:10; and Colossians 1:4, 9-10.

If asking for the intercession of Christians in heaven (the saints) takes away from Christ's unique mediation, as the challenge proposes, then what is Paul doing encouraging intercession from Christians on earth? Wouldn't that, too, detract from Christ's unique mediation? No Christian wants to affirm that conclusion. Most Protestants, like Catholics, pray for and request prayers from their fellow Christians all the time. Since this biblical practice doesn't conflict with Christ's role as a unique mediator, neither does requesting prayers from the saints in heaven.

A second reason why Jesus' unique mediation as the God-man doesn't prevent us from asking the saints to intercede on our behalf is that he is able to share that ministry with others. According to Matthew 23:8, Jesus is our unique "teacher," (Greek, *didaskalos*), yet there are many who participate in his teaching ministry, as seen in Ephesians 4:11 and James 3:1. Jesus is our one "high priest," as per Hebrews 3:1, yet, according to 1 Peter 2:5 and 9, we're all priests (albeit of a different kind) insofar as we are Christians.

The same principle could apply to the intercession of the saints. Of course, Jesus is the one mediator, and he "always lives to make intercession," as Hebrews 7:25 says. But that doesn't mean he can't share that intercessory role with his saints.

In fact, we know that he does share that intercessory role with at least some of his saints: the Christians here on earth. (*Saints* is a word commonly used in the New Testament for all Christians, as seen, for example, in 2 Cor. 1:1, Eph. 1:1, Phil. 1:1). Paul urges Timothy in 1 Timothy 2:1 that "intercessions… be made for all men."

Therefore, it's at least possible that Jesus could share his intercessory ministry with Christians in heaven, too.

Third, the saints participate in Christ's unique mediation because they're members of the mystical body of Christ. As quoted above, Paul teaches in his first letter to the Corinthians that we as Christians are "baptized into one body" (v. 13), which he identifies as "the body of Christ" (v. 27). Christians are united with one another in the body by virtue of their union with the head, Jesus. This union with Christ enables the intercessory prayer of Christians to bring about effects in the lives of other members in the body. As the *Catechism* states in paragraph 2635, "Christian intercession participates in Christ's."

Viewed this way, we see that intercessory prayer of one member of Christ's mystical body for another no more takes away from Christ's unique mediation than the individual parts of my body take away from the overall function of my body. It is only because of my life that the different members of my natural body can aid one another for a proper functioning of the whole. Similarly, it's because of Christ the head that different members of his body can intercede for one another.

Rather than detracting from the head, the intercession among members of his body manifests the head's glory.

The saints in heaven are still members of Christ's mystical body. We know this because Paul teaches in Romans 8:35 and 38 that death is among his list of things that cannot separate us from "the love of God which is in Christ Jesus."

And the saints are not just average members of Christ's body; they are "the spirits of just men made perfect," as Hebrews 12:23 puts it. This matters because James tells us in James 5:16 that "the prayer of a righteous man has great power in its effects." Since the saints in heaven are perfected in righteousness, their prayers will bear much fruit.

So what did Paul mean in 1 Timothy 2:5 if he wasn't denying mutual Christian intercession? He's highlighting the *uniqueness* of Jesus' intercession, which is twofold. First, Jesus is the *only* God-man, and thus the only one who can give human beings access to God the Father. Second, he's the *only* mediator of the New Covenant (Heb. 8:6, 9:15, 12:24), the way Moses was the mediator of the Old Covenant (Gal. 3:19). Nobody else—not even any other Christian—is a mediator in these senses.

> **The Book of Hebrews teaches that there is only one *heavenly* intercessor.**

A Protestant might counter this argumentation and say, "Your response misses the mark. We're not concerned with *earthly* mediation taking away from Christ's unique mediation. We're concerned only with the claim that there are other *heavenly* intercessors."

Take, for example, Lutheran pastor and professor of systematic theology Jordan Cooper. In his online video, "A Critique of Prayer to the Saints," he argues that the Book of Hebrews' description of what's going on before the Father in the heavenly throne room doesn't "leave room at all for a kind of other heavenly intercession."[67]

There are two ways that we can respond to this argument. One is more general, which considers Cooper's argument itself. The other is more specific to what Cooper says elsewhere in his video.

Here's the general response. Recall, Cooper's argument says there can be no other heavenly intercessor because that role belongs to Jesus alone, who has ascended into the heavenly sanctuary to minister as our high priest. But isn't the Holy Spirit a heavenly intercessor as well? Paul says he is:

> The Spirit helps us in our weakness; for we do not know how to pray as we ought, but the Spirit himself *intercedes for us* with sighs too deep for words. And he who searches the hearts of men knows what is the mind of the Spirit, because the Spirit *intercedes for the saints* according to the will of God (Rom. 8:26-27).

Cooper's logic would have us deny the heavenly intercession of the Holy Spirit, which is something we can't accept as Christians. Given that Cooper's logic leads to a direct denial of Paul's explicit teaching about the Holy Spirit's heavenly intercession, his argument fails.

Now, Cooper might counter, "Of course the Holy Spirit can intercede for us because he's consubstantial with the Son— that's to say, he's identical in being with the Son. The heavenly intercession that I'm concerned with is *creaturely* intercession."

But if *creaturely* intercession in heaven is the problem, then we'd have to reject the heavenly intercession of the elders (human souls—see chapter two) in Revelation 5:8 and the angel in Revelation 8:3-4. Recall what John sees in Revelation 5:8:

> And when he had taken the scroll, the four living creatures and the twenty-four elders fell down before the Lamb, each holding a harp, and with golden bowls full of incense, which are the prayers of the saints.

In Revelation 8:3-4, John describes an angel doing the same thing:

> And another angel came and stood at the altar with a golden censer; and he was given much incense to mingle with the prayers of all the saints upon the golden altar before the throne; and the smoke of the incense rose with the prayers of the saints from the hand of the angel before God.

As we argued in chapter three, the term "prayers of the saints" in both passages refers to Christians on earth. And the elders and the angel are presenting their prayers to the Lamb, Jesus, in the heavenly throne room. That's *heavenly* intercession, performed by *creatures*.

If the elders in Revelation 5:8 and the angel in Revelation 8:3-4 can be heavenly intercessors without taking away from Christ's unique mediation as our heavenly high priest, then so can the saints. There is in fact enough "room" (to use Cooper's words) in the heavenly throne room for multiple intercessors, especially when those other intercessors intercede with Christ by virtue of their union with Christ through grace.

Now, concerning our more specific response, Cooper contradicts himself in his video. In the above argument, he restricts heavenly intercession to Christ. Yet, later in the video, when commenting on the elders in Revelation 5:8 (see above), he concedes that they intercede for us in a general way, saying, "Certainly they are before God; it is likely that the saints in heaven pray for the church."[68] Which is it? Is it Christ *alone* who intercedes in heaven, or do the elders intercede as well? That's something for Cooper to answer.

Catholics violate the Bible's prohibition to communicate with the dead.

Besides the objection from Christ being the one mediator in 1 Timothy 2:5, the claim that Catholics violate the Bible's prohibition against communicating with the dead ranks at the top. Deuteronomy 18:10-12 is the key text. It reads,

> There shall not be found among you any one who burns his son or his daughter as an offering, anyone who practices divination, a soothsayer, or an augur, or a sorcerer, or a charmer, or a medium, or a wizard, or a necromancer. For whoever does these things is an abomination to the Lord; and because of these abominable practices the Lord your God is driving them out before you.

For some Protestants,[69] it couldn't be clearer: the Bible explicitly rules out the Catholic practice of invoking the saints. It's not only unbiblical; it is "abominable."

One way we can answer this objection is to say Deuteronomy 18:10-12 is condemning not communication with the dead, but the practice of conjuring the spirits of the dead with a desire to gain hidden or supernatural knowledge apart from God. The Merriam-Webster online dictionary defines *necromancy* as "conjuration of the spirits of the dead for purposes of magically revealing the future or influencing the course of events." The term comes from two Greek words: *nekros* ("dead person") and *manteia* ("oracle," "divination").

There are at least two reasons why eliciting supernatural knowledge or oracles from the dead is what Deuteronomy 18:10-12 has in mind. First, the text also forbids "divination" and seeking a "medium," a "sorcerer," and a "wizard," all of which have to do with an attempt to gain knowledge beyond ordinary human intelligence. The Hebrew biblical phrase *doresh'el-hametim*, which is translated as *necromancer*, literally means "an inquirer of the dead."[70]

The second reason is the subsequent instructions Moses gives concerning a coming prophet. In verse 15, Moses says, "The Lord your God will raise up for you a prophet like me from among you, from your brethren—him you shall heed." In other words, there is no need to go to mediums, sorcerers, wizards, and necromancers to gain knowledge because God will send a prophet of his own. God then speaks through Moses and says in verse 18, "I will put my words in his mouth, and he shall speak to them all that I command him." As for the prophet who presumes to speak in God's name without God's command or the prophet who speaks in "the name of other gods," God says in verse 20 that that prophet "shall die."

Since the context is about looking to God's prophet for divine oracles and not to mediums, sorcerers, wizards, and necromancers, it's clear that the prohibition has to do with conjuring up the dead to seek supernatural knowledge apart from God (necromancy), not *speaking* or *communicating* with the dead.

Now, the Catholic practice of invoking the saints to pray for us simply *isn't* necromancy. Asking saints to pray for us is an entirely different thing from necromancy. The Church doesn't teach that we are to invoke the saints by conjuring their spirits to gain secret knowledge or knowledge of the future apart from God—in fact, this is condemned in paragraph 2116 of the *Catechism*. Since the Catholic practice of petitioning the saints to pray for us is not a form of necromancy, it doesn't fall under the prohibition in Deuteronomy 18:10-12.

Now, a Protestant might counter and say, "You're misrepresenting the objection. I'm not excluding communicating with the dead in *any* context. I'm only arguing against communication with the dead when the contact *originates with us*." This seems to be Protestant apologist James White's argument when he deals with this topic in his book *Answers to Catholic Claims: A Discussion of Biblical Authority*. He writes, "The only communication with spirit beings that originates with man that is allowed in Scripture is that of prayer to God and he alone."[71]

How might we respond to this counter?

First, an appeal to Deuteronomy 18:10-12 still wouldn't justify the claim that we can't initiate communication with the dead in the way that Catholics do when we invoke them for their prayers. Recall, necromancy is the "*conjuration* of the spirits of the dead *for purposes of magically revealing the future or influencing the course of events*." That's not what we do when we ask the saints to pray for us, even if we're initiating some sort of communication with them—namely, making our request known to them. We do not *conjure* the spirits, nor do we contact them *for the purposes of giving us secret knowledge about the future* or for the sake of influencing the course of events apart from God's will.

Second, Peter initiates communication with the dead when he raises the young girl Tabitha. We're told in Acts 9:40 that

Peter turned to Tabitha's dead body and said, "Tabitha, rise up." If Peter, a Christian here on earth, can initiate contact with the dead by commanding the soul to be reunited with its body, then it's at least permissible for us Christians to initiate contact for something far less dramatic: a simple request for prayers.

A third response, and our last one here, is that the Bible reveals that we Christians *do* in fact initiate some sort of contact with the blessed in heaven. Consider, for example, Hebrews 12:18-24. The author writes,

> You have not come to what may be touched, a blaz-
> ing fire, and darkness, and gloom, and a tempest [Mt.
> Sinai]....But you have come to Mount Zion and to
> the city of the living God, the heavenly Jerusalem, and
> to innumerable angels in festal gathering, and to the
> assembly of the first-born who are enrolled in heaven,
> and to a judge who is God of all, and to the spirits of
> just men made perfect, and to Jesus, the mediator of a
> new covenant, and to the sprinkled blood that speaks
> more graciously than the blood of Abel.

The author is contrasting the Old and New Covenants here. In the New Covenant, we approach the "spirits of just men made perfect" at the same time we approach Jesus "the mediator of a new covenant." Some have interpreted this as a reference to what we're approaching when we pray. Regardless, it's clear that we initiate some sort of contact with the blessed in heaven in something similar to the way we initiate contact with Jesus.

Now, someone might counter, "Your defense of initiating contact with the dead conflicts with what your Church teaches about *spiritism*—the practice of contacting the dead. After absolutely prohibiting divination, which involves practices that are 'supposed to unveil the future,' 'whether through recourse to Satan or demons, conjuring up the dead' (CCC 2116), the *Catechism* has this to say about spiritism: 'Spiritism often implies divination or magical practices; the Church for her part warns the faithful against it' (2117). Invoking a saint to pray for you seems to fall under spiritism because, like with divination, you're initiating contact with the dead."

It's true that divination *involves* contact with the dead. But the *Catechism* is not envisioning the logical content of divination to be identical to contact with the dead. Rather, the *Catechism* identifies "divination" with "[having] recourse to Satan or demons, *conjuring up the dead* or other practice falsely supposed to 'unveil' the future."

So, in paragraph 2117, the *Catechism* isn't condemning contacting the dead in an *absolute* sense. Rather, it's condemning contact with the dead when such contact involves divination or magical practices.[72] As Jimmy Akin asks, "What if you contact them but you *don't* do divination or magic?" It would seem, assuming that all else is proper and good, at least from the Church's perspective, that this would be permitted.

The *Catechism* doesn't seem to be making an absolute prohibition against spiritism, but merely providing a strong warning against it due to its frequent association with divination and magic. Given that our invocation of the saints' intercession doesn't involve divination or magic, it's not a prohibited form of contacting the dead.

The Bible never instructs us to pray to the saints.

Whenever we're talking about whether it's appropriate to ask the saints to intercede for us, an objection that's inevitably made is, "The Bible never instructs us to pray to the saints, or make our request known them. Therefore, we shouldn't do so."[73]

The first thing we can say in response is that this objection commits a fallacy known as *negating the antecedent*. Negating the antecedent refers to when a person poses a hypothetical, "If A, then B"; negates the first part of the statement (called the *antecedent*), "not A"; and concludes, "Not B."

For example, it's true that if it's raining outside, then the ground is wet. But let's suppose we deny the first part of the statement and say, "It's not raining outside." Can we conclude, "The ground is not wet"? Of course not, since the ground may be wet due to some other reason, like leaving the outside faucet on.

The objection we're considering here follows this same line of reasoning. It assumes that *if* the Bible gives us an instruction to behave in a certain way, *then* we should do it. We agree 100 percent here.

But notice that the objection denies the first part of the statement, saying, "The Bible *doesn't* give instruction to ask the saints to pray for us," and concludes, "We shouldn't ask the saints to pray for us." This reasoning is not at all different from the example with rain and a wet ground.

Now, our Protestant friend might rephrase his objection this way:

P1: We should confine our religious practice only to what the Bible instructs us to engage in.

P2: Invoking the saints' intercession is not a religious practice that the Bible instructs us to engage in.

C: Therefore, we shouldn't engage in the religious
       practice of invoking the saints' intercession.

Unlike the first attempt, this line of reasoning is valid. The
conclusion follows from the premises.

But the problem here is premise one. It assumes that the
Bible is the *only* source for knowing which religious practices
we should engage in as Christians. But how do we know this?
Nowhere does the Bible tell us this.

A Protestant may respond with an appeal to 2 Timothy 3:15-
16, where Paul tells Timothy, "All Scripture is inspired by God
and profitable for teaching, for reproof, for correction, and for
training in righteousness, that the man of God may be complete,
equipped for every good work."

But affirming that the Bible is "profitable," or helpful, to
achieve all these things doesn't mean it's the *only* thing we need
to accomplish these things. St. Paul tells us in 2 Thessalonians
2:15 that there are some traditions handed down by word of
mouth that we need to hold fast to.

Another possible response is that the Bible is simply the only
infallible rule of faith that we have left, given that all the apostles
died and their apostolic authority with them.[74] But this runs
into a couple of problems.

First, if the Bible were the only infallible rule of faith left,
then a Protestant would be in a dilemma concerning having
certain knowledge as to whether certain books in the Bible are
inspired, since several of them are never revealed by Jesus or the
apostles to be inspired by God.

Jesus doesn't give us a detailed list of which Jewish or Christian writings are divinely inspired. We might be able to deci-
pher a general and vague knowledge of which Jewish writings
he judged to be inspired (Matt. 4:4/Deut. 8:3; Matt. 22:32/

Exod. 3:6), but he doesn't give us very much. For sure, we can't discern which Christian writings are inspired by looking to Jesus, because he never talked about such writings.

Now, the apostles do tell us a few things that can lead to infallible knowledge as to which Christian writings are inspired. (We'll leave the Jewish writings aside to keep things simple.) Peter, for example, refers to Paul's writings as "scripture" (2 Pet. 3:16), which means that Peter believed they were divinely inspired. That covers quite a bit of the New Testament.

Another example is Paul's quotation of a passage from Luke's Gospel (Luke 10:7) in 1 Timothy 5:18, which Paul introduces as "for the Scripture says." This tells us that Paul believed, at least, that *this* passage from Luke is divinely inspired. And I suppose we can be generous and infer from Paul's statement that the *whole* of Luke's Gospel is also inspired.

The problem, however, is that the apostles say *nothing* about the rest of the writings that Christians believe to be divinely inspired—i.e., the New Testament canon (for both Catholics and Protestants). For example, they don't tell us that the Gospel of Mark is inspired, which is a problem because Mark wasn't even an apostle.

A Protestant might counter and say that Mark was the scribe of Peter. And given that Peter was infallible by virtue of his apostolic authority, it follows that the content of Mark is infallible by virtue of Peter. But Peter never tells us, through Mark, that the content in Mark's Gospel is divinely *inspired*. That's what we're after here.

Moreover, no apostle ever teaches us when an apostle is under divine inspiration. So just because Peter is behind the content of Mark's Gospel, that doesn't necessarily mean that the actual words of Mark's Gospel are inspired.

Furthermore, we don't know who wrote the Book of Hebrews. This being the case, we can't lump it under Paul's writings, which Peter calls "scripture." Sure, there is scholarship behind throwing the Book of Hebrews in with Paul's epistles. But there is also scholarship against it. Ultimately, we don't really know. And no apostle ever tells us that it's inspired, much less apostolic.

And what about the epistle of James? No apostle ever tells us that James's epistle is divinely inspired. That belief doesn't appear, seemingly, until Origen in the mid-third century (*Commentary on Romans*, 4.8.2). James's epistle is definitely *apostolic*, though. But, again, no apostle ever tells us that whatever an apostle writes automatically is divinely inspired.

Now, recall that the above objection states that there are no other infallible sources for Christian belief and practice besides Scripture. In other words, the infallible authority that the apostles had is no longer available to us as Christians because they all died. According to Protestants, the apostles didn't transfer their infallible authority to other men. This means we're left *only* with Scripture as our infallible rule for Christian belief and practice.

So if we were to follow the line of reasoning that the Bible is our only infallible rule of faith, the divinely inspired nature of *some* Jewish and Christian writings would be beyond what we could infallibly know—that's to say, we couldn't infallibly know whether some books belong in the Christian canon of Scripture.

There's a second problem with the above Protestant counter-response: it's not consistent with the Bible and early Christian sources. Both the Bible and early extra-biblical Christian sources make it clear that one way the Holy Spirit preserved the apostolic traditions was by leading the apostles to appoint men to succeed them in their apostolic ministry, and they charged such men with preserving what the apostles had taught. For example, before his death, Paul arranged for the Apostolic Tradition to be passed on in the post-Apostolic Age. He tells Timothy, "What you have *heard* from me before many witnesses entrust to faithful men who will be able to teach others also" (2 Tim. 2:2).

We also have evidence from extra-biblical Christian sources that the apostles appointed men to succeed them for the sake of preserving what they taught. Clement of Rome's first-century letter to the Corinthians (c. A.D. 70) is one example. He writes,

> Our apostles also knew, through our Lord Jesus Christ, that there would be strife on account of the office of the episcopate. For this reason, therefore, inasmuch as they had obtained a perfect foreknowledge of this, they appointed those [ministers] already mentioned [bishops—at chapter 42], and afterward gave instructions, that when these should fall asleep, other approved men should succeed them in their ministry.[75]

Irenaeus of Lyons, a bishop of the late second century, affirms that the apostolic traditions were preserved in this line of succession from the apostles. Here's what he writes in his classic work *Against Heresies*:

> It is within the power of all, therefore, in every church, who may wish to see the truth, to contemplate clearly the tradition of the apostles manifested throughout the whole world; and we are in a position to reckon up those who were by the apostles instituted bishops in the churches, and [to demonstrate] the succession of these men to our own times; those who neither

taught nor knew of anything like what these [here-tics] rave about.[76]

For Irenaeus, the truth of Apostolic Tradition is preserved in the succession of bishops from the apostles. This is what we find in Scripture.

Must we conclude that the Holy Spirit inspired Paul and the early apostles to appoint men to succeed them in their apostolic teaching ministry only for those successors to be left without the aid of the Holy Spirit to preserve them in the truth? Given the evidence above, it's more reasonable to conclude that the infallible teaching authority of the apostles didn't die with the apostles. Rather, it continued in the men they chose to succeed them, called bishops.

Given that premise one in the above argument isn't true, the argument doesn't work. As such, that the Bible doesn't give us explicit instruction to ask the saints to pray for us should not be a reason for someone to think it's not appropriate to ask the saints in heaven to pray for us.

A second thing we can say in response is that even though there's no explicit instruction for us to pray to the saints, we can still *infer* the practice from what's divinely revealed. This is a method that most Protestants should have no problem with.

Protestant apologist Gavin Ortlund, for example, in a 2023 debate with Trent Horn, argued that looking only to the Bible for Christian belief and practice is a "good and necessary conse-quence" of *sola scriptura*, the Protestant doctrine that the Bible is the Christian's only infallible rule of faith. Others argue this, too.[77] When it comes to "all things necessary for his own glory, man's salvation, faith and life," the Westminster Confession of Faith states that such things are "either expressly set down in

Scripture, or *by good and necessary consequence may be deduced from Scripture.*"[78]

Although we're not directly instructed to invoke the saints for their prayers, it's something that fits within the "good and necessary" category. Consider, for example, what we said above concerning Paul's instruction in 1 Corinthians 12:20-21 not to refuse help from other members of the mystical body of Christ: "There are many parts, yet one body. The eye cannot say to the hand, 'I have no need of you,' nor again the head to the feet, 'I have no need of you.'"

Since the saints in heaven are still members of the body of Christ (remember that according to Romans 8:35 and 38, death doesn't separate us from the love of God in Christ Jesus), it is a "good and necessary" consequence that at least we ought not reject their help that's offered through their intercessory prayer. And if we can't reject it, then it would be a good Christian practice to employ it.

We can also infer the instruction to invoke the saints' intercession by appealing to the revelation that they *in fact* intercede for us. Recall from chapter two that Revelation 5:8 reveals human souls in heaven offering to Jesus the petitions of Christians on earth. God's revealing such activity implies that it is permissible for us to make our requests known to the saints.

This line of reasoning is like our justification for praying to the Holy Spirit. Nowhere does the Bible give explicit instruction to pray to the Holy Spirit. But given that Paul says in Romans 8:26-27 that the Holy Spirit intercedes for us, we can infer that it is permissible for us to pray to him. Many Protestants agree with this.

Another way we can infer the instruction to request the saints' prayers is from Paul's request in Romans 15:30 that the Romans intercede for him: "Strive together with me in your prayers to God on my behalf, that I may be delivered from the unbelievers in Judea, and that my service for Jerusalem may be acceptable to the saints."

Paul sees the Christian life as involving requests made for other Christians to intercede on our behalf. That's what Christians do. Therefore, since the saints in heaven are Christians in the perfect sense, and they do in fact pray for us, we can infer that the Christian life involves making requests for Christians in heaven to pray for us.

So, even though the Bible doesn't give explicit instruction to request the saints' intercession, it gives us enough information about the saints that justifies our requests for their intercession.

A third response to the above argument is that of apologist Jimmy Akin, which he gives in his book *A Daily Defense*. Things that are not prohibited by Scripture and have a rational basis are permitted under Christian liberty. Asking the saints to pray for us is nowhere forbidden in the Bible. Such a practice has a rational basis, as we've shown above. Therefore, asking the saints to pray for us is permitted under Christian liberty. This kind of liberty fits well with the "freedom which we have in Christ Jesus" that Paul describes in Galatians 2:4.

Finally, if we're going to follow the principle of the above argument and reject religious practices because Christians have never received explicit instructions to engage in them, then we're going to have to reject multiple Christian practices that most Protestants approve of. For example, the New Testament never instructs us to reject certain lifestyle choices, like transgenderism. Sure, the rejection of transgenderism is a "good and necessary consequence" of biblical teaching—namely, that God made the first humans male and female, identities defined by the role such humans perform in the reproductive act. But there's no *instruction* to reject these lifestyle choices, as there is for drunkenness or homosexuality. If the rejection of transgenderism can be a good and necessary consequence of Scripture, as most Protestants would affirm, then so can the invocation of the saints.

Also, the New Testament never instructs us to use instruments in Christian worship. It instructs us to sing, but it lacks instructions for instruments.

Some Christians bite the bullet here and stay true to the principle, excluding instruments from their services.[79] But most Protestants find this too restrictive. So, if we can use instruments for Christian piety without instruction, then why not the invocation of the saints?

Now, a Protestant might counter and say that when it comes to the use of instruments for worship, we at least have the Old Testament approving their use (e.g., Ps. 150:3-5—"trumpets," "harps,""timbrels,""strings and pipes," and "cymbals"; 2 Samuel 6:5—"harps, lyres, tambourines, sistrums, and cymbals"). But those pro-instrument passages speak of *specific kinds* of instruments. How would we discern as Christians whether *other* kinds of instruments, like pipe organs, guitars, drums, etc., are permitted, given that we have no instructions concerning them? If we follow the logic embedded in the above argument, we'd have to reject the use of such instruments.

Another Christian practice that the Bible—whether Old Testament *or* New Testament—never instructs Christians to engage in is congregating on Sundays. If a Christian were to reject the invocation of the saints because the Bible never instructs us to do so, then he would have to reject the Christian practice of congregating on Sundays. There are some who are fine with this proposal (e.g., Seventh-Day Adventists). But most aren't!

A possible counter here is that such a practice is *rooted* in the New Testament, given that the first-century Christians assembled on "the first day of the week [Sunday]" to "break bread" (Acts 20:7). As a response, this counter shifts to a different problem concerning the invocation of the saints. Initially, the problem was that the invocation of the saints lacked evidence from the Bible giving *instruction* to invoke the saints. The above counter, however, makes a different problem—namely, a lack of evidence of the early Christian *practice*. This leads to the next argument.

> ### There is no evidence in the New Testament of the actual practice of invoking saints.

Given the arguments above, a Protestant might be willing to give us a pass on the need to provide biblical evidence for the *instruction* to invoke the saints. But he won't give us a pass when it comes to providing examples in the New Testament of the early Christians engaging in such a practice. If invoking the saints is something we should be doing as Christians, so it might be argued, then there should be at least some *examples* in the New Testament of the early Christians doing it. Since there are no such examples, invoking the saints is not something that we should be doing as Christians.

This objection is guilty of the same fallacious reasoning, of negating the antecedent, as in the above argument. It assumes that *if* there is New Testament evidence of an early Christian practice, *then* we should do it. We couldn't agree more.

But notice that the objection we're considering here denies the first part of the above conditional, saying, "There is *no* New Testament evidence of the early Christian practice of invoking the saints" and concludes, "We shouldn't ask the saints to pray for us." We are back to rain and a wet ground.

Now, our Protestant friend might rephrase his objection this way:

P1: We should confine our religious practices only to Christian practices that we find in the New Testament.

P2: Invoking the saints' intercession is a religious practice that we do not find the early Christians practicing in the New Testament.

C: Therefore, we shouldn't engage in the religious practice of invoking the saints' intercession.

Again, we are back to square one, with a valid line of reasoning undone by a false premise. Here is the problem: nowhere do the apostles teach that we must confine our religious piety only to practices found in the New Testament. Moreover, Protestants engage in religious practices that aren't found in the New Testament. For example, no one in the New Testament prays the "Sinner's Prayer." ("Dear Lord Jesus, I know I am a sinner, and I ask for your forgiveness. I trust and follow you as my Lord and Savior.") As Protestant apologists Matt Slick and Tony Miano explain, "there is not a single verse or passage in Scripture, whether in a narrative account or in prescriptive or descriptive texts, regarding the use of a 'Sinner's Prayer' in evangelism. Not one."[80]

There are also no examples in the New Testament of Christians marrying each other with a formal ceremony, involving witnesses and formal vows. Yet Protestants see such practices as something good and necessary not just for civil purposes, but for religious purposes as well.

There is no New Testament evidence of a Christian invoking the angels in heaven. Yet one Protestant doxology does this very thing: "Praise him above, ye heavenly host." If Protestants can invoke the angels without a New Testament precedent, then why can't we invoke the saints?

Now, a Protestant might counter, "Well, we at least have an Old Testament precedent in Psalm 103:20: 'Bless the LORD, O you his angels, you mighty ones who do his word, hearkening to the voice of his word!'" But if Jewish precedents are permitted as justification for Christian practices, then we're safe with invoking the saints. When Jesus cries on the cross, "My God, my God, why have you forsaken me?", St. Matthew tells us that those present at the cross thought Jesus was calling out to Elijah, saying, "This man is calling Elijah…let us see whether Elijah will come to save him" (27:46-49). According to the logic of the above counter, this Jewish belief in the legitimacy of invoking Elijah's help would justify the invocation of the saints as a Christian practice.

Here's yet another Christian practice that lacks evidence in the New Testament: Christians engaging in the private reading of the scriptures. Must we reject this Christian practice because we have no evidence from the New Testament of Christians engaging in it? Of course not!

"But we have the example of the Ethiopian eunuch," a Protestant might argue. In response, the Ethiopian eunuch was not a Christian. *He* may have been doing it, but that doesn't mean it's okay for a *Christian* to do it.

In fact, we might think that this text counts against the private reading of Scripture. The evangelist Phillip interrupts the private reading and gives the eunuch the necessary instruction. This fits with St. Peter's teaching that the prophecy of Scripture is not a matter of private interpretation (2 Pet. 1:20) and that Paul's letters are hard to understand, which some twist to their own destruction (3:15-16).

We may get the impression from these texts that private reading of Scripture is something *not* rooted in the New Testament and even discouraged. This is not to say that private reading of Scripture is something we shouldn't do. Rather, it's simply to point out that the Ethiopian eunuch's private reading doesn't work in a Protestant's favor for the religious practice of reading Scripture in private.

Speaking of devotional reading of the scriptures, implicit in a Protestant's practice of such reading is the acceptance of their sixty-six-book biblical canon. But this too is something that lacks evidence in the New Testament. If we must reject the invocation of the saints because there is no New Testament example of Christians engaging in such piety, then a Protestant must reject his pious acceptance of the sixty-six-book canon. Indeed, he can't accept *any* number of books in the canon, because there's no example of such a pious practice. Surely, no Protestant wants to do that.

Finally, there is no evidence of the early Christians using instruments in their worship services. Paul says they sang hymns (1 Cor. 14:26) but says nothing about instruments. Must we reject the use of instruments in our worship services, given this lack of evidence? Some follow the logic and say yes. But most would say no. If we can use instruments in our worship services without mention of it in the New Testament, then we can invoke the saints.

> ## There is no evidence of the practice from the first- and second-century Fathers.

A critic of the invocation of the saints may be willing to allow for a lack of evidence in the New Testament, given its limited scope. The New Testament authors weren't trying to give an exhaustive treatise on Christian faith and practice. It's reasonable, therefore, to expect a lack of evidence for some Christian practices.

But it might be argued that there should at least be some evidence in the extra-biblical Christian sources from the first or second century. For example, the New Testament lacks evidence of Christians invoking angels. But Hermas invokes angels in *The Shepherd*,[81] thus justifying the Protestant practice in the above-mentioned Protestant doxology: "Praise him above, ye heavenly host."

Gavin Ortlund takes this approach in his YouTube video "Praying to the Saints: A Protestant Critique."[82] He states,

> Our concern is that [the invocation of the saints] is a historical accretion, a historical innovation. Something that gradually comes into the picture and not authentically related to the first-century and biblical instruction and Jesus' teaching.

Ortlund's implication here is that we ought not to engage in the practice of invoking the saints because of this concern. Ortlund's argument, therefore, amounts to the following:

P1: If a Christian practice is not found within the first two centuries of Christianity, then we shouldn't engage in it.

P2: Invoking saints is a Christian practice that is not
    found in the first two centuries of Christianity.

C: Therefore, we shouldn't invoke the saints.

The key premise to challenge is premise one, and there are
several different ways that we can do this. First, by what authority does Ortlund claim that a Christian practice shouldn't be
adopted if there is no evidence of it occurring before the end
of the second century?[83] It's a bit arbitrary to say the end of the
second century is the cutoff date for lack of evidence. Why not
the end of the third century?

Second, this objection embodies the same logic as the previous objection. The difference is that in the previous objection,
the appeal was to a lack of evidence in the New Testament,
whereas in this objection, the appeal is to a lack of evidence in
the writings of the first- and second-century Church Fathers.
The similarity in the logic calls for a similar response: there are
several practices that Protestants engage in that aren't found in
the first- and second-century Fathers—again, as above, like
weddings with vows and ministers, or the private reading of
Scripture.[84]

The practice of referring to the epistle of James as inspired
is also not found in the first- and second-century Fathers. As
mentioned above, that doesn't happen, seemingly, until Origen
in the mid-third century (*Commentary on Romans*, 4.8.2).

The *good* use of musical instruments in Christian worship
services is yet another example. Clement of Alexandria does
mention their liturgical use in his *Instructor* (A.D. 198), but such
use is viewed in a *negative* light.[85] When he speaks positively of
using instruments to play godly music, it's outside the context
of liturgical worship.[86]

So Protestants have adopted several religious practices that aren't mentioned in the first- or second-century Fathers. Will they follow the logic of the present objection and reject them? Perhaps, but I wouldn't bet on it.

There's one more way that we can respond to premise one. Notice that the implied principle is that we ought to reject any religious practice that's not found in the first and second centuries. The question is, why? For most Protestants, a lack of such evidence proves that such a practice is a historical "accretion" or "innovation," and thus not part of historic Christian life.

But lack of evidence of the invocation of the saints in the first and second centuries doesn't mean it wasn't part of the historic Christian faith. First- and second-century sources for Christian life are scarce. It's unreasonable to think that all the aspects of Christian life wouldn't go beyond the boundaries of such a limited pool of sources. Furthermore, there may very well have been early records of the practice, and they're simply lost to us.

Now, a Protestant might counter and say that the silence in the first- and second-century Christian sources that we do have is an unexpected silence. In other words, it's reasonable to think that the sources we do have would mention the invocation of the saints if it were part of historic Christian life.

For example, Gavin Ortlund argues that the honor expressed for Polycarp in the *Martyrdom of Polycarp* would have been a perfect place for Christians to invoke his prayers.[87] Similarly, Jordan Cooper thinks Irenaeus's response to the Gnostics, who believed in divine beings that populated heaven, called *aeons*, would have been a fitting place to mention the practice of invoking the saints, redirecting the Gnostics' belief in the aeons as intermediaries to the true intermediaries—the saints.[88]

Concerning the *Martyrdom of Polycarp*, its focus is the *martyrdom* of Polycarp, not what the Christians did or didn't do after his martyrdom. They may have invoked his prayers later, and it's just not mentioned in the document.

Cooper's argument from Irenaeus is not any more persuasive. The aeons weren't exactly intermediaries in the way that Christians think the saints in heaven are. They were supernatural divine beings, vastly superior to humans. (One of them made the material world.) If Irenaeus had tried to offer the Gnostics the saints in place of the aeons, the Gnostics would have been gravely tempted to think the saints were not at all different from their aeons. The risk of idolatry would have been too high. Thus, *contra* Cooper, this context is not a fitting place for Irenaeus to mention the invocation of the saints, and therefore there is no need to expect that he would.

Now, let's assume for argument's sake that the invocation of the saints *wasn't* a Christian practice in the first and second centuries and, in the words of Ortlund, was a "historical accretion." Why must we reject a religious practice that's not concretely part of early Christian life?

Just because a religious practice wasn't a practice of Christians in the early centuries doesn't mean it's not Christian in nature. As we showed above, the invocation of the saints is based on principles revealed in the New Testament. Thus, the invocation of the saints is Christian *in nature*. And if that's the case, then such a practice can be adopted as part of Christian life.

Moreover, given that such a practice is based on principles contained in the revealed data, it's possible that the early Christians were not engaging in the practice because they had not yet thought through the implications of the revealed data, given their focus on the prior and more fundamental truths, such as

Christ's divinity, the mystical union believers have with Christ and one another as believers, etc.

We can't expect implications of the fundamental truths of revealed data to be in full force when such fundamental truths are the focus. Implications of revealed data, like the invocation of the saints, take time to be teased out of the data and thought through. Thus, we might even say that we shouldn't be surprised that we don't find the invocation of the saints within the first two centuries of Christianity and that it's unreasonable to demand that it be there.

All the above responses have taken for granted that there's no evidence for the invocation of the saints in the first and second centuries. But such a claim, which is premise two in the above argument, can be reasonably challenged. It's true that we don't have any *direct* evidence that Christians in the first two centuries invoked the saints. But a case can be made for *indirect* evidence.

Recall from above the mid-third-century evidence for the invocation of the saints: the *Sub Tuum Praesidium* hymn (230-250), the early Christian grave inscription that invokes Gentianus for his intercession (250), and the *Memoria Apostolorum*—the catacomb inscriptions invoking Ss. Peter and Paul. These invocations were not presented as a novelty. They appear as part and parcel of Christian life and piety. It's not that much of a stretch to say that such practices would have been present a mere fifty years before. If so, that would put the practice of invoking the saints' intercession at the end of the second century. Maybe premise two in the above argument is not true after all.

**We don't need the saints.
We can go straight to Jesus.**

When talking about the Catholic practice of asking the saints to pray for us, a question arises from both Catholics and Protestants: "Why seek the help of saints when we can go straight to Jesus?" Protestants often pose this question as an objection. For Catholics, it's a question of curiosity.

There are two ways to answer. The first is to address the problematic assumptions, which we would direct primarily at our Protestant friends who ask this question as an objection. The second, which can be directed at both Protestants and Catholics, is to give positive reasons for the practice.

Let's look at the assumptions first.

Consider that many who ask this question assume that the Catholic practice of asking the saints to pray for us implies that we *can't* go straight to Jesus. But nothing could be further from the truth. The Catholic Church affirms wholeheartedly that we can go straight to Jesus in prayer. The *Catechism* teaches in paragraph 2665,

> The prayer of the Church, nourished by the word of God and the celebration of the liturgy, teaches us *to pray to the Lord Jesus*. Even though its prayer is addressed above all to the Father, it includes in all the liturgical traditions forms of prayer addressed to Christ.

Notice that the Church *doesn't* say we *must* invoke the saints to pray for us before we can go straight to Jesus. The Church affirms that Christians have a straight path to Jesus.

A second, common assumption is that we should not seek the saints' help *because* Jesus' intercession is sufficient. Now, it's true that Jesus' intercession is sufficient, as the Catholic Church affirms in paragraph 662 of the *Catechism*. The Church teaches that Christ, in the heavenly sanctuary, "permanently exercises his priesthood, for he 'always lives to make intercession' for 'those who draw near to God through him,'" quoting Hebrews 7:25.[89]

But this shouldn't be the reason why our Protestant friends reject seeking the saints' prayers. If Jesus' sufficiency as our intercessor *precluded* our asking the saints in heaven to pray for us, then there'd be no reason to ask the "saints" on earth (born-again Christians) to pray for us, either. The same question could be asked: "Why seek the help of Christians on earth when we can go straight to Jesus?"

No Christian wants to say we shouldn't pray for one another. Therefore, the sufficiency of Jesus' unique intercession doesn't serve as an obstacle to the invocation of the saints' intercession.

Now let's look at some positive reasons why we should seek help from the saints.

First, it's God's will, and it has positive consequences. God has determined that he will answer some requests when multiple people are praying, which he might not answer if fewer people were to pray.

Second, since it's God's will for the saints to pray for us, our asking their intercession gives glory to God. And it gives glory to God not just because it's his will. Our request for the saints' intercession gives God glory because, as we mentioned in a previous chapter and above in this chapter, it highlights his goodness and wisdom in willing to use the saints to help us.

A third positive reason for the practice of the invocation of the saints is that St. Paul instructs us not to refuse help from other members of the mystical body of Christ. We've covered 1 Corinthians 12:20-21 a couple of times already, and it bears repeating again here: "There are many parts, yet one body. The eye cannot say to the hand, 'I have no need of you,' nor again the head to the feet, 'I have no need of you.'"

Now, the saints in heaven are still members of the body of Christ. Paul teaches us in Romans 8:35 and 38 that death doesn't separate us from the love of God in Christ Jesus.

Since Christ has willed that we not reject the help of other members of the body of Christ, and the saints in heaven are members of the body of Christ, it follows that we shouldn't deny their help that's offered through their intercessory prayer. We should employ it, since we need all the help we can get.

Given that the saints are fellow Christians, invoking their intercession is in principle not at all different from Paul in Romans 15:30 asking the Christians in Rome to pray for him: "Strive together with me in your prayers to God on my behalf, that I may be delivered from the unbelievers in Judea, and that my service for Jerusalem may be acceptable to the saints." Why should where Christians exist (earth or heaven) be an obstacle to requesting their prayers, especially when such prayers are empowered by Jesus' unique mediation, no matter where they're offered?

A fourth reason, and the final one we'll consider here, is that the saints' prayers bear much fruit, as St. James makes clear in James 5:16 when he writes about the prayers of a righteous man. We know that the saints in heaven are perfectly just. The author of Hebrews, in 12:22-23, writes, "You have come to…the heavenly Jerusalem…to the spirits of just men made perfect." Therefore, the prayers of the saints in heaven have great power in their effects.

Going straight to Jesus for help is essential to the Christian life. But going to other members of his mystical body for help, including those perfected members in heaven, is not to be disregarded. It's the Christian way.

The practice of invoking the saints has led to abuses and violations of the gospel.

Gavin Ortlund makes this objection in his video, "Praying to the Saints: A Protestant Critique." He argues that when we consider "how the prayers to the saints actually played out" in medieval piety, we discover that the practice led to many distortions.[90]

Ortlund gives several examples. I can't quote them all. But here are some relevant excerpts that include the *primary* "distortion" that causes him concern:[91]

> "Lord, we ask that thou, *placated by the intercession of all thy saints*…We pray thee, Lord, that the merits of blessed Mary, who is both perpetually a virgin and the bearer of God, may attend us and always *implore thy forgiveness for us*." [*Cursus Honorum* of the Blessed Virgin Mary, According to the Ordinarium of the Church of Hildeshelm].

> "O noble Mary, excellent above all, *procure for us forgiveness*."

> "O holy virgin Mary, and all the saints and elect of God, come to aid me, wretched one, now and in the hour of my death, and *make the Lord our God propitious to me by your merits and prayers*."

> "*Through you forgiveness is granted* to the guilty" [Sequence to Our Lady and Sequence in Praise of the Virgin].

For Ortlund, the above invocations are "inherently wrong" and are in "error" because the *soteriology* (that is, the study of salvation) embedded within them is flat-out contrary to the gospel of Jesus Christ. As he puts it, "it is subtracting from the sufficiency of Christ because the specific tasks that are the property of Christ in the gospel are being assigned to Mary here." Which tasks? Procuring the forgiveness of sins and propitiating or placating God, which, for Ortlund, can be done only by the death of Jesus on the cross.

It's because of these distortions, Ortlund explains, that Protestants, including himself, are concerned with the practice of invoking the intercession of the saints. And such a concern is good enough reason for him not to engage in the practice, at least when combined with the lack of New Testament and early Christian evidence that Christians requested that the saints in heaven pray for them.

We covered already the supposed lack of early evidence for invocations. Here, we will focus on Ortlund's concern about these so-called distortions, and his reasoning about them.

Assuming for argument's sake that these requests are distortions, notice how Ortlund concludes that we shouldn't invoke the saints' help *because such invocations have played out in a way that violates the Bible's teaching on salvation*—namely, that we are forgiven for our sins through the merits of Jesus' death on the cross.

Now, one might think that Ortlund is guilty of committing the *association fallacy*, which asserts that the quality of *some* things within a category (when not essential to those things) is a quality of *all* things within that category. If Ortlund were to conclude that *all* invocations of the saints *are* violations of the gospel because *some* are, then he would be guilty of fallacious reasoning. But Ortlund simply argues that such invocations *can lead to* violations, and on this basis, he chooses not to engage in the practice.

But why should we reject the invocation of the saints simply because *some* invocations *lead to* a violation of the gospel (again, assuming that the above invocations truly are violations of the gospel)? We don't reject interpreting Scripture just because some interpretations lead people to destruction (2 Pet. 3:15-16). Nor do we reject the practice of religion simply because some who practice it do so in a way that leads to unjust conflict and violence.

Concerning the interpretation of Scripture, we realize that it's not the interpretation of Scripture itself that leads to destruction. Rather, it's specific interpretations and whatever method the interpreter is using. Similarly, when it comes to religion, we recognize that it's not religion itself that leads to conflict and violence. Rather, it's the perversion of religion by the one causing unjust conflict and violence.

The same line of reasoning applies to the so-called "distorted" invocations of the saints. Ortlund, or anyone, for that matter, shouldn't reject the practice of invoking the saints on these grounds because it's not the practice of invoking the saints itself that is the problem. In the examples Ortlund gives, it would be the specific requests themselves that are "distorted" and the soteriological beliefs that are driving these specific requests. And if that's the case, there's no need for Ortlund to persuade others away from the practice of invoking the saints for their intercession. There could be some invocations that are not problematic and worthy of Christian practice.

Now, this response assumes that the requests in the above excerpts are actual "distortions." But we have good reason to think they're not.

Recall that Ortlund is concerned with the invocations because they take away from the sufficiency of Christ insofar as they attempt to procure the forgiveness of sins from and propitiate or placate God. Notice the hidden assumption: *nobody except Christ can procure the forgiveness of sins from God or propitiate or placate him.*

If by "procure," Ortlund has primary causality in mind, then we agree. *Only* Christ is the efficient cause of the forgiveness of sins. But that's not how the above excerpts should be read. The "procuring" is by way of request. In other words, the above prayers are simply asking Mary to pray that God will forgive us our sins.

Is it okay for Mary to do this? Well, it's not at all different from Paul praying, "May the Lord grant [Onesiphorus] *to find mercy* from the Lord on that Day [the Day of Judgment]" (2 Tim. 1:18). If Paul can pray for a Christian to be forgiven by God, so can Mary. And if it's okay for Mary to do this, then the above requests made of Mary are not "distortions" of the gospel.

Concerning the request that Mary would propitiate or placate God, all this entails is a request that Mary would ask God to be more favorable to us. If Paul and Mary can ask God to forgive our sins, which is just *one* way in which God can be favorable to us, then Paul and Mary can ask God to be favorable to us in other ways.

Moreover, the Bible reveals that we can participate with God in making others more favorable for salvation. Consider Paul's teaching as to how a believing spouse can contribute to the salvation of an unbelieving spouse:

> If any woman has a husband who is an unbeliever, and he consents to live with her, she should not divorce him. For the unbelieving husband is consecrated

> through his wife, and the unbelieving wife is conse-
> crated through her husband.…Wife, how do you
> know whether you will save your husband? Husband,
> how do you know whether you will save your wife?
> (1 Cor. 7:13-14, 16).

If believing spouses can "procure" salvation for their unbelieving spouses through cooperating with God, then Mary can
"procure" salvation for us, too.

As much as I appreciate Ortlund's honest and charitable
expression of his concerns with the Catholic practice of the
invocation of the intercession of the saints, when thought
through, the concern dealt with here doesn't justify a rejection
of invoking the saints. Not only are the requests in the excerpts
above not violations of the gospel, which is a major motivation
behind Ortlund's concern, but his reasoning is fallacious even
if we grant that these requests are perversions. If Ortlund wants
to justify his rejection of the practice of invoking the saints,
he's going to have to ground his rejection in better arguments.

The Catholic doctrine of the intercession of the saints involves the false doctrine of merit.

Concerning the intercession of the saints, the *Catechism* teaches,

> Being more closely united to Christ, those who dwell
> in heaven fix the whole Church more firmly in holi-
> ness.…They do not cease to intercede with the Father
> for us, as they proffer the merits which they acquired
> on earth through the one mediator between God and

men, Christ Jesus....So by their fraternal concern is
our weakness greatly helped (956).

For some Protestants, the problem with the doctrine of the
intercession of the saints is not so much asking a perfected
Christian in heaven to pray for us here one earth. Rather, the
problem is the doctrine of *merit*, which is tied to the Catholic understanding of the intercession of the saints.[92] For these
Protestants, the doctrine of merit is contrary to Scripture. Since
the invocation of the saints according to Catholic belief entails
such a doctrine, they conclude that the invocation of the saints
is contrary to Scripture.

The first thing that we can say in response is that this would
be a reason to reject only one aspect of the Catholic doctrine
of the intercession of the saints. It's not a reason to reject the
intercession of the saints in its entirety.

Second, the doctrine of merit is biblical. Consider, for example, Paul's teaching that wages are received in proportion to our
labor: "He who plants and he who waters are equal, and each
shall receive his wages according to his labor (1 Cor. 3:8)."

The labor that Paul speaks of here is not ordinary manual
labor. Rather, he's talking about *laboring for God* as "God's fellow
workers" "building upon" the foundation, which is "Jesus" (vv.
9, 11). The wages that he speaks of are rewards that a person
receives *in heaven*. That they're conceived of as rewards is shown
in verse 14: "If the work which any man has built on the foundation survives, he will receive a reward." And that the rewards
are received in heaven is indicated by Paul saying that such an
individual will "be *saved*" (v. 15).

Paul's teaching on merit abounds:

Galatians 6:7–9: "Whatever a man sows, that he will also reap. For he who sows to his own flesh will from the flesh reap corruption; but he who sows to the Spirit will from the Spirit reap eternal life. And let us not grow weary in well-doing, for in due season we shall reap, if we do not lose heart."

Romans 2:6–7: "For he will render to every man according to his works: to those who by patience in well-doing seek for glory and honor and immortality, he will give eternal life."

2 Corinthians 5:10: "For we must all appear before the judgment seat of Christ, so that each one may receive good or evil, according to what he has done in the body."*

Finally, the idea that the saints take their merit with them into heaven has biblical roots. Take, for example, Revelation 14:13: "Blessed are the dead who die in the Lord henceforth. 'Blessed indeed,' says the Spirit, 'that they may rest from their labors, for *their deeds follow them*!'" If the saints' deeds follow them into heaven, then surely the rewards for those deeds (see Rom. 2:6-7 above)—namely, their merit—follow them as well. And if that's the case, then they can apply those merits to other Christians. Describing the interrelationship of members of Christ's mystical body, Paul writes, "If one member is honored, all rejoice together" (1 Cor. 12:25).

---

* Hebrews 11:6 is another passage that we could include in the list *if* we assume with some biblical scholars that Paul wrote Hebrews. It reads, "He [God] rewards those who seek him."

Given that the doctrine of merit is biblical, along with the idea of the exchange of spiritual blessings among members of Christ's mystical body, the Catholic association of merit with the saints' intercessory prayer shouldn't be a reason to reject the Catholic doctrine of intercession of the saints or our invocation of them.

CHAPTER 5

It's Good to Venerate Them

"Honoring the saints," also called the *veneration* of the saints (coming from the Latin word *venerārī*, which means "to revere" or "to honor"[93]), covers a variety of Catholic practices. It can refer to the interior honor, or respect, that we give a saint in our heart or to exterior acts of honor directed to them that involve their relics and images—bowing, kissing, reservation in sacred spaces, etc.

This practice of honoring the saints, and in particular honoring them with images, was first dealt with by the Second Council of Nicaea (787), the Seventh Ecumenical Council of the Catholic Church. In response to those who were rejecting and destroying the images of saints (called *iconoclasts*), the council declared,

> We, following the royal pathway and the divinely inspired authority of our holy fathers and the traditions of the Catholic Church (for, as we all know, the Holy Spirit indwells her), define with all certitude and accuracy that just as the figure of the precious and life-giving cross, so also the venerable and holy images, as well in painting and mosaic as of other fit materials, should be set forth in the holy churches of God, and on the sacred vessels and on the vestments and on hangings and in pictures both in houses and by the wayside, to wit, the figure of our Lord God and Savior Jesus Christ, of our spotless Lady, the Mother of God, of the honorable angels, of all saints and of all pious people. For by so much more frequently as they are seen in artistic representation, by so much more readily are men lifted up to the memory of their prototypes, and to a longing after them.[94]

The Council of Trent affirmed this infallible teaching in response to Protestants who at the time were pushing their own iconoclasm, accusing Catholics of "idol worship." The council declared,

> The holy synod enjoins on all bishops, and others who sustain the office and charge of teaching, that, agreeably to the usage of the Catholic and Apostolic Church, received from the primitive times of the Christian religion, and agreeably to the consent of the holy fathers, and to the decrees of sacred councils, they especially instruct the faithful diligently concerning... *the honor [paid]* to relics [of the saints]; and the legitimate *use of images* [of the saints]...that the holy bodies

of holy martyrs, and of others now living with Christ, which bodies were the living members of Christ, and the temple of the Holy Ghost, and which are by him to be raised unto eternal life, and to be glorified, are to be *venerated by the faithful*; through which [bodies] many benefits are bestowed by God on men; so that they who affirm that veneration and honor are not due to the relics of saints; or, that these, and other sacred monuments, are uselessly honored by the faithful; and that the places dedicated to the memories of the saints are in vain visited with the view of obtaining their aid; are wholly to be condemned, as the Church has already long since condemned, and now also condemns them.

Moreover, that the images of Christ, of the Virgin Mother of God, and of the other saints, are to be had and retained particularly in temples, and that *due honor and veneration* are to be given them; not that any divinity, or virtue, is believed to be in them, on account of which they are to be worshiped; or that anything is to be asked of them; or, that trust is to be reposed in images, as was of old done by the Gentiles who placed their hope in idols; but because *the honor which is shown them is referred to the prototypes that those images represent*; in such wise that by the images that we kiss, and before which we uncover the head, and prostrate ourselves, we adore Christ; and *we venerate the saints, whose similitude they bear*: as, by the decrees of councils, and especially of the second Synod of Nicaea, has been defined against the opponents of images.[95]

There are several different facets to the veneration of the saints. There is the practice of honoring them in *general*, which involves holding them in high esteem and looking to them as models of the Christian life. Then there is the concrete honor we show them by reverencing their relics and images.

In this chapter, we will deal with the honor that we show the saints in general, reserving veneration of relics and religious images for chapters six and seven. Our defense in this chapter will include both positive and negative arguments—arguments in support of the practice of showing honor generally and arguments that refute objections posed to the practice. Let's get started!

Arguments in Favor

There are two arguments that we can propose in favor of the veneration of the saints in general. One appeals to the *Church's articulation* of the difference between the honor that we give God and the honor that we reserve for his creatures perfected in grace—i.e., the saints. The other roots the general practice of honoring the saints in the Bible, showing that the principle of giving higher honor to some of God's holy ones is revealed in the New Testament.

From the distinction between *dulia* and *latria*

The Catholic Church has defined the essential difference between the honor we give to God through prayer and the honor we give to the saints. The Second Ecumenical Council of Nicaea (787) defined the "adoration" we give to God alone as *latreia* (Greek) or *latria* (Latin).

The use of this term has its roots in Scripture. For example, in Galatians 5:20, the "idolatry" that Paul condemns translates the Greek word *eidololatria*, which means "image worship, idolatry."[96] The author of the letter to the Hebrews uses the Greek word *latreias* when he speaks of the "ritual duties" that the Old Testament priests perform (9:6).

In order to distinguish the honor that we give the saints from the honor that belongs to God alone (adoration), the council fathers chose the term *douleia* (Greek) or *dulia* (Latin). In Scripture, the Greek word *dulos*, from which *douleia* is derived, is often translated as *servant* (Matt. 10:24) or *slave* (Eph. 6:8). It signifies service given by one human to another.

It's this sense of human deference of one to the other that belongs to the essence of the honor we give to saints when we pray to them, also referred to in Catholic theology as *veneration*. The council's Doctrinal Declaration reads as follows:

> The more frequently they are seen in representational art, the more are those who see them drawn to remember and long for those who serve as models, and to pay these images the tribute of salutation and respectful veneration. Certainly this is not the full adoration [*latria*] in accordance with our faith, which is properly paid only to the divine nature, but it resembles that given to the figure of the honored and life-giving cross, and also to the holy books of the gospels....Further, people are drawn to honor these images with the offering of incense and lights, as was piously established by ancient custom. Indeed, the honor paid to an image traverses it, reaching the

model, and he who venerates the image, venerates the person represented in that image.[97]

Some Protestants, however, don't buy this line of reasoning. They argue that this distinction is not grounded in Scripture. Take, for example, Protestant apologist James White. He writes,

> When we come to the New Testament…we discover that there is absolutely no distinction made between [*dulia* and *latria*] relevant to religious worship.
>
> As an example, we note Galatians 4:8: "However at that time, when you did not know God, you were slaves [Greek, *edouleusate*] to those which by nature are no gods." But when you did not know God, you served [footnote 22: *edouleusate*—from *douleuō*, the verb form of *dulia*], or were slaves to, those which by nature are not gods.
>
> Paul is speaking of the former idolatry of the Galatians. They served (*dulia*) idols, those which by nature are not gods at all. Are we to assume, then, on the basis of the Roman Catholic definitions, that since they only served these idols that they were free from the charge of idolatry, since they didn't give *latria* as well? Of course not! Their service of these idols was wrong whether the term *latria* or *dulia* was used.…
>
> No matter how the defender of Rome tries, no basis can possibly be found in Scripture for the distinction of *latria* and *dulia*.[98]

One problem with White's objection is that he seems to assume that a Catholic would deny that the Greek word *edouleusate* is being used in reference to the Galatians formerly worshiping idols. But that's not the case. Catholics recognize that the service (*douleia*) the Galatians gave the false gods was idolatry.

The question is not whether the Greek word *douleia* (and the terms related to it) can be used in reference to the service or worship we give God. The question is whether *douleia* and *latreia* can be validly distinguished.

First, we may note that the Greek verb *douleuō* is also used in reference to *human* service.

For example, in the Septuagint, Deuteronomy 15:18 features the verb *douleuō* to describe the role of a hired servant: "It shall not seem hard to you, when you let him go free from you; for at half the cost of a hired servant he has served [Greek, *edouleusen*] you six years." *Douleuō* (and thus *douleia*), therefore, can represent the service of one human to another.

The number of times the New Testament uses a related noun, *doulos*, for a human "servant" is too large to list all of them here. A simple look at a biblical concordance reveals as much (e.g., Matt. 8:9, 13:28).

So the Bible uses *douleia* and its related words *both* for service given to other humans and for service given to God or the gods.

This is true of other, related words. Consider the Greek verb *proskuneō*, for example, which means "to express in attitude or gesture one's complete dependence on or submission to a high authority figure, (fall down and) worship, do obeisance to, prostrate oneself before, do reverence to."[99]

This word is used for the *worship* that the twenty-four elders offer to the Lamb in Revelation 5:14. Yet it's also used in Revelation 3:9 to refer to those of the synagogue of Satan whom

Jesus will make bow down before Christians: "I [Jesus] will make those of the synagogue of Satan…come and bow down [Greek, *proskunēsousin*] before your feet."

What these examples reveal is that it's not the word itself that determines whether the act of bowing is one of worship or not. It's the one to whom the action is directed and the intention with which the act is being performed.

In the case of *douleia*, it constitutes divine worship or adoration when the object of service or honor is God, or at least what one thinks is a deity. When it's another human, and that human is treated as such, then it's the honor due to a creature. As seen in the case of *proskuneō*, if the object of the service or honor is God, then we take it to mean adoration. If it's a creature, and the intention behind the action is creaturely honor, then it's not adoration.

By contrast, the term *latreia* is used both in the Greek Old Testament and in the New Testament, where it is *always* used to refer to the worship of God or the gods. For example, in John 16:2, Jesus says that some who put Christians to death will think they are offering "service [*latreia*] to God," and in Romans 12:1, St. Paul says we should present our bodies to God as a living sacrifice for this "is your spiritual worship [*latreia*]."

As a result of this exclusive use in Scripture, *latreia* came to be associated closely with divine worship among Christians, whereas *douleia* could still be used with reference to humans. In later centuries, the Church decided to formalize this distinction and mandate that the term *latreia* (*latria* in Latin) be used for divine worship and *douleia* (*dulia* in Latin) be used for mere veneration.

This is similar to how Christians took other terms and gave them more precise meanings than they had in Scripture. For example, in later theology, terms like *the elect* came to refer to those people who will be saved on the Last Day. However, in Scripture the term had a more general meaning and referred to those who were chosen by God to have a special relationship with him—not specifically those who would be saved in the end.[100]

Language changes over time, and situations can arise in which terms need to be given precise definitions to avoid theological confusion. When the Church needed to develop a precise way of expressing the distinction between divine worship and human veneration, it chose *latreia* for the former—since it was used in Scripture to express divine service—and it chose *douleia* for the latter—since it could refer to merely human service.

The Catholic Church, therefore, has grounds for making the distinction it does between the honor given to saints (*dulia* in Latin) and the adoration given to God (*latria* in Latin). Whereas *dulia* can apply to the honor given to God or other entities who aren't God, depending on the context, *latria* applies only to honor given to God.

> **From the biblical principle that establishes honoring God's holy ones and distinctions among degrees of honor.**

There are two aspects of the practice of honoring the saints: the *general* honor given to all of God's holy ones and the *degrees* of honor that are shown to some and not others. Concerning the general honor shown to God's holy ones, the evidence abounds.

Take, for example, Elizabeth's proclamation of Mary's blessedness: "Blessed are you among women, and blessed is the fruit of your womb" (Luke 1:42). Elizabeth gives us an example of the honor that is owed to Mary as Mother of God.

But not only do we have an example of honor being given to Mary, but we also have instruction from Mary herself to do so: "For behold, henceforth all generations will call me blessed; for he who is mighty has done great things for me, and holy is his name" (Luke 1:48). No argument from a lack of instruction can be given here, like what we saw above in response to the invocation of the saints.

Now, it's not just Mary whom we're instructed to honor. There are others. Consider, for example, Paul's instruction that we must honor fellow Christians: "Love one another with brotherly affection; outdo one another in *showing honor*" (Rom. 12:10).

Paul seems to be taking his cue from Jesus: "If anyone serves me, the Father will honor him" (John 12:26). If the Father honors the saints, then so can we. Moreover, we *should* honor the saints because such respect is due to them. Honoring those who believe in Christ, therefore, is part and parcel of the Christian life.

Showing *differing degrees* of honor is also part and parcel of Christian practice. For example, Paul instructs Timothy, "Let the elders who rule well be considered worthy of *double honor*, especially those who labor in preaching and teaching" (1 Tim. 5:17). Similarly, Paul instructs the Thessalonians, "Respect those who labor among you and are over you in the Lord and admonish you [bishops and elders], and...esteem them very highly in love because of their work" (1 Thess. 5:13).

So honoring other members of Christ's mystical body, and even honoring some more than others, is biblically based, and revealed to be part of historic Christianity.

Arguments Against

When it comes to the honor that we show the saints, most Protestants will not have any quarrels with honoring them in the sense of respecting them and looking to them as models for the Christian life.[101] The problem really comes with the *concrete ways* in which we honor them: "praying to them" and reverencing their images and relics. As mentioned above, we will deal in the next two chapters with arguments against honoring the saints via their images and relics. In this chapter, we will look at an argument that challenges the practice of "praying to" the saints as a form of honor.

Doesn't "praying to the saints" make gods out of them?

For Catholics, invoking the saints, or what is often called "praying to the saints," is an act of honor. But for some Protestants, such an act of honor makes the saints into gods because the English word *pray* is often associated with the communication we have with God in modern American English.[102] Others argue on the grounds that in the Greek text of the Bible, the main verb for "pray," which is *proseukhomai*, and the equivalent noun for "prayer," which is *proseukhe*, are used exclusively to refer to communication with God or the gods.[103] The assumption here is that we should model our language of "prayer" on the way the Bible uses it.

How should we respond?

It's important to point out, as apologist Jimmy Akin does,[104] that the language of "praying to the saints" is language that's never used by the Catholic Church's Magisterium. Rather, the more common language in official Church documents is "the invocation of the saints" (see, for example, CCC 969).

So a Catholic could say in response that the objection doesn't have any bearing on what the Church *actually* teaches and go on his merry way.

But the objection still presents a problem for Catholics who use the lingo of "praying to the saints." Should Catholics drop this lingo and restrict their use of "prayer" to how the Bible uses it?

It's true that we should frequently stick to the way faith-related terms are used in the Bible. But language does change and develop with time.

Consider, for example, the word *Bible*, which is based on the Greek term *biblion*. *Biblion* originally didn't refer to what we mean today by *bible*—a collection of individual books that we consider inspired. Rather, it referred to a sheet of papyrus and later came to mean things like "letter," "document," and "scroll."

Another example of religious vocabulary that's developed from its biblical usage by theological communities is the phrase *the elect*. In both Catholic and Protestant communities, *the elect* refers to all those who will be saved on the Last Day. But as some have pointed out,[105] that's a *post*-biblical usage, since in Christian usage, "the elect" or "the chosen" refers to all Christians who from eternity have been chosen to have a special relationship with God. Such a relationship is viewed in light of Israel's relationship with God in the Old Testament.

The term *pray* is yet another example of a biblical term that has developed over time in its use. It has its roots in the Latin verb *precare*. *Precare* means "to ask," "to beg," "to implore," "to entreat," "to supplicate," etc.

In Latin, *precare* is used both for asking God or the gods for things and for asking other human beings for something. Both these uses carried over into English.

Webster's Dictionary defines *prayer* as follows:

1) An address (such as a petition) to God or a god in word or thought

2) An earnest request or wish

Notice that although *prayer* can denote an act of worship, the word is not restricted to that definition. It has a wider meaning of earnest request, including requests made to non-divine beings. It's this sense of the term that Catholics intend when we speak of *praying* to the saints.

The Catholic use of the term here is similar to how it was used in older forms of English: "pray tell" or "I pray thee, my lord." Those translations of the Bible that use older forms of English, such as the Catholic Douay-Rheims Bible (DRE) and the Protestant King James Bible (KJV), provide us with some examples, such as 1 Kings 2:17-20. In verse 17, Adonijah (son of David, Solomon's half-brother) requests that Bathsheba speak to King Solomon on his behalf: "I *pray* thee speak to King Solomon (for he cannot deny thee anything)" (DRE). Obviously, Adonijah was not engaging in an act of worship directed to Bathsheba. He was making an earnest request.

The same language is used subsequently to describe the request that Bathsheba makes of King Solomon: "I desire one small petition of thee; I *pray* thee, say me not nay" (v. 20, KJV). Like Adonijah, Bathsheba was making a petition, not worshiping the one to whom the petition was made.

Similarly, Catholics *pray* to the saints only in the sense that we *petition* them for intercessory prayer. Our Protestant friends might not be comfortable with Catholics using this sort of language, but at least we can see that it's justified, given its established use in English-speaking communities. What's most important is what we *mean* by the term and its implications.

Petitioning the saints in heaven is indeed an act of honor. But it is not the honor due to God alone. It is an honor that each member of the body of Christ is worthy of, given the fact that Christ wills members of his mystical body to help one another. Paul writes, you'll recall, that "the eye cannot say to the hand, 'I have no need of you,' nor again the head to the feet, 'I have no need of you'" (1 Cor. 12:21).

As mentioned above, the Catholic Church has defined the essential difference between the honor we give to God through prayer and the honor we give to the saints. The Second Ecumenical Council of Nicaea (787) defined the "adoration" we give to God alone as *latreia* (Greek) or *latria* (Latin). We already saw above how the use of this term has its roots in Scripture.

The council fathers chose the term *douleia* (Greek) or *dulia* (Latin) to refer to the honor that we give to the saints. And we saw how such a word is used in Scripture to signify service given by one human to another. It's this sense of human deference of one to the other that belongs to the essence of the honor we give to saints when we pray to them.

The honor we give to the saints is grounded in the honor that God the Father gives them: "If anyone serves me, the Father will honor him" (John 12:26). If the Father honors the saints, then so can we. And since requesting the saints' intercession is an act of honor that is not adoration, it follows that we can request their intercessory prayer without such a petition being an act of worship.

The Second Vatican Council's Dogmatic Constitution on the Church *Lumen Gentium* speaks of the "cult" of Mary.

Some Protestants might have a hard time buying our above argument concerning the honor that we give to the saints because the Second Vatican Council's Dogmatic Constitution on the Church *Lumen Gentium* speaks of both the "cult of the saints" and the "cult of Mary." Concerning the saints, it states, "Let [the bishops]…teach the faithful that the authentic *cult of the saints* consists not so much in the multiplying of external acts, but rather in the greater intensity of our love" (51).

Then, in sections 66-67, the council fathers dedicate an entire section to Mary entitled "The Cult of the Blessed Virgin Mary in the Church." It states, "Placed by the grace of God, as God's mother, next to her Son, and exalted above all angels and men, Mary intervened in the mysteries of Christ and is justly *honored by a special cult in the Church*."

Given these statements from Vatican II, it would *seem* that the honor we give the saints is an honor that belongs to God alone. But this is based on a misunderstanding of the term *cult*.

The term *cult* comes from the Latin *cultus,* which has multiple meanings—"care," "worship," "devotion/observance," or "training/education."[106] It's the "worship" meaning that the above objection latches on to. However, it fails to recognize that the term can rightly be used simply to refer to devotional practices or observances that manifest honor or respect due to a creature. This meaning is recognized even by modern dictionaries.

This is the meaning with which the council fathers used *cultus* as regards Mary and the saints. After referring to the "cult of the saints," the council fathers distinguish such devotion from the worship that we give to God, stating,

> Let [the bishops] teach the faithful that our commu-
> nion with those in heaven, provided that it is under-
> stood in the fuller light of faith according to its
> genuine nature, in no way weakens, but conversely,
> more thoroughly enriches the *latreutic worship* we give
> to God the Father, through Christ, in the Spirit (51).

The council fathers here employ the term used by the Second Council of Nicaea for the devotion that is due to God alone: *latria.* And notice that they *exclude* from such "latreutic worship" devotions that make up the "cult of the saints."

Such a distinction is also made with the "cult of Mary." Again, the council fathers state,

> This cult, as it always existed, although it is altogether
> singular, *differs essentially from the cult of adoration* [*cultu
> adorationis*] which is offered to the incarnate Word, as
> well to the Father and the Holy Spirit, and it is most
> favorable to it" (66).

The "cult of Mary," therefore, along with the "cult of the saints," is not to be considered a "cult of adoration." When read in light of the intended meaning of the council fathers, such language need not be an obstacle to the practice of honoring the saints.

CHAPTER 6

It's Good to Venerate Them with Images

A s mentioned above, for some Protestants the general honor that we show the saints by looking to them for imitation and inspiration is not the problem.[107] Rather, it's the *concrete ways* in which we honor them. In our previous chapter, we looked at the practice of "praying to" the saints. Another such practice that's perceived to be a problem is veneration or reverence of the saints' images.

Now, there are two general forms of reverence showed to the images of saints. First, we simply *have* them and *look upon* them with devotion in the heart. Second, we engage in pious *acts* in which we reverence the image—what theologian Ludwig Ott calls "acts of veneration," like kissing an image, bowing before an image, burning candles before an image, or incensing an image.[108]

The arguments below both in favor of and against the veneration of religious images will be divided according to the above two forms of reverence.

Arguments in Favor

As mentioned, we can divide our arguments in favor of the veneration of the saints' images into two categories: arguments for *having* religious images and arguments for the *veneration* of religious images. The kinds of arguments for both categories are biblical and theological in nature.

Arguments for *Having* Images of the Saints

From the Bible

There are several instances in the Bible where God commands the construction of religious images, and in particular religious images reserved for places of worship. Consider, for example, the two golden sculptures of cherubim that God orders in Exodus 25:18-20 to be put on the lid of the Ark of the Covenant. God also instructs that cherubim be woven into the curtains of the tabernacle in 26:1. When God in 1 Kings 6:23-29 gives instructions for building the Temple during the reign of King Solomon, he commands that two fifteen-foot tall cherubim statues be placed in the holy of holies and that "figures of cherubim" be carved into the walls and doors of the Temple.

Later, in 1 Kings 9:3, we read that God approves of such things, saying to Solomon, "I have consecrated this house which you have built, and put my name there forever; my eyes and my heart will be there for all time." God's blessing on the Temple is certain evidence that he approves of having statues and religious images in places of worship.

Another example where God commands the making of a statue is in Numbers 21:6-9. The Israelites are suffering from venomous snakebites. To heal them, God instructs Moses to construct a bronze serpent and set it on a pole so that those who have been bitten can look upon it and be healed. Again, God approves of having images within a religious context—the religious context being obedience to God's command.

There's one more path that we can take for arguing from a biblical perspective. Consider what John says in Revelation 5:8 of the blessed in heaven: "When he had taken the scroll, the four living creatures and the twenty-four elders fell down before the Lamb, each holding a harp, and with golden bowls full of incense, which are the prayers of the saints."

Here, John uses signs and symbols made of *ink* to represent or call to mind the blessed in heaven. If it's okay for John to use ink for such an end, then shouldn't it be okay for Christians to use signs and symbols made of stone, wood, marble, etc. for the same end?

St. John Damascene uses a similar argument in his *Exposition on the Orthodox Faith* concerning the events of Christ's life—except he goes further than defending the written word, and explicitly defends pictures:

> Seeing that not everyone has a knowledge of letters nor time for reading, the Fathers gave their sanction to depicting these events [the events of Christ's life] on images as being acts of great heroism, in order that they should form a concise memorial of them.[109]

If we can depict the life of Christ with images, then we can depict the life of those who imitated him (the saints) with images.

From spiritual benefits

Not only do we have biblical precedent for the use of religious images, but we also have practical reasons.

First, the saints' images instruct us in the Christian faith. As Damascene says in the above quote, for those who were not able to read, or just didn't have the time, they were instructed about the mysteries of Christ's life through images representing such mysteries. Now, if images can serve the purpose of instructing us about Christ's life, then they can serve to instruct us about the lives of the saints, which are in themselves concrete manifestations of how to live the Christian life. To deny the use of the saints' images is to deny an important means of instruction in the Christian faith.

Second, the images of saints help us remember to give them the honor that is due them. As the common saying goes, "Out of sight, out of mind." There's a lot of truth to this. We tend to forget things that are not constantly set before us. Thus, if we live our Christian lives without the saints' images, we may be inclined to forget about them, and thereby forget to give them the honor they're due.

Third, the images of saints remind us of *our* intended final destiny: heaven. Without constant reminders of our ultimate destination, we may be inclined to forget about it and pursue goals without subordinating them to it.

Fourth, as we constantly look upon the images of the saints, we're reminded not only of where they are, but also how they got there: by living a life of virtue and holiness.

Arguments for *Venerating* Images of the Saints

From being physical beings

We are not mere spirits. We are embodied spirits, having both a soul *and* a body. Consequently, our interior acts of will are visibly expressed in our bodily acts. And such bodily acts are the acts of the person *himself*.

This is why we kneel when we pray to God, and sometimes even prostrate ourselves. The bodily act is an act of humility and worship because it visibly manifests the interior act of the will to worship God as Creator. Consider, for example, how when fire came down from heaven and consumed the burnt offerings and sacrifices after Solomon's prayer in 2 Chronicles 7:1-3, "all the children of Israel saw the fire come down and the glory of the LORD upon the temple, they *bowed down with their faces to the earth* on the pavement, and worshiped and gave thanks to the LORD." They perceived that they needed to worship in a bodily way, prostrating themselves down before the presence of Yahweh. Such a bodily gesture visibly manifests our humility before God.

The Psalmist recognizes the need to visibly manifest in the body his interior act of worship by *turning toward* the Temple when he prays. He writes, "I through the abundance of your merciful love will enter your house, I will worship toward your holy temple in the fear of you" (Ps. 5:7).

This idea of expressing the invisible through bodily acts is also seen in acts of repentance. For example, when Joshua and the elders repent on behalf of Israel, they "*tore [their] clothes*, and *fell to the earth upon [their] face* before the ark of the LORD until the evening . . . and they *put dust upon [their] heads*" (Josh. 7:6).

141

It's this understanding of the human person as a body-soul composite that grounds our visible acts of veneration or honor offered to the saints, such as bowing before their images, kissing their images, and other pious acts of reverence. They *visibly* express the interior act of our will to honor the saints whom the images represent. Sure, we *could* honor the saints merely with our interior act of the will. But then we wouldn't be engaging our full human nature. Why not honor the saints in a *fully* human way?

From veneration of the ark, the bronze serpent, and the Temple

The idea of venerating holy objects with bodily acts of veneration is not foreign to the Bible. Consider, for example, the Ark of the Covenant. The Israelites venerated the ark in a few different ways—first, by not touching it; otherwise, they'd die.[110] This was done in obedience to God's command: "They must not touch the holy things [including the ark], lest they die" (Num. 4:15; see also 2 Sam. 6:6-7). Notice that they reverenced the other holy items from the holy dwelling of God by not touching them. Can you imagine what a Protestant might think if Catholics were to refrain from touching an image of Mary, lest they die? "Illicit veneration" would be the Protestant's battle cry. And yet that would be in line with Scripture!

Second, the Israelites' priests and army venerated the Ark of the Covenant during the procession around the walls of Jericho.[111] God gives instruction to Joshua for the priests to blow their "trumpets of rams' horns before the ark" (vv. 4-5) and for "the armed men [to] pass on before the ark of the Lord" (v. 7). Again, imagine the pope commanding Catholics to use an image of Mary as they go to battle a foreign enemy and play musical instruments in honor of Mary as they march. The charges of "idolatry" would resound within Protestant echo chambers. And yet, again, the Bible seems pretty sympathetic to it.

There's another holy object in the Old Testament that the Israelites venerated: the bronze serpent (Num. 21:4-9). Not only were they commanded to erect the bronze serpent, but they were also commanded to *look upon it for healing*:

> The LORD said to Moses, "Make a fiery serpent, and set it up as a sign; and everyone who is bitten, when he sees it, shall live." So Moses made a bronze serpent, and set it up as a sign; and if a serpent bit any man, he would look at the bronze serpent and live (vv. 8-9).

To intentionally look upon the bronze serpent for healing is a visible act of veneration.[112] If God commands his people to venerate or honor material objects of the Old Covenant consecrated unto the Lord—the Ark of the Covenant and the bronze serpent—then why would God be opposed to his people in the New Covenant venerating or honoring material objects that represent human beings who are perfectly consecrated unto the Lord—the saints in heaven? The answer is that he wouldn't.

Finally, the Jews venerated the holy Temple itself with bodily acts of veneration.[113] Consider the Psalmist, for example. He writes, "I *bow down toward* your holy temple and give thanks to your name for your mercy and your faithfulness" (Ps. 138:2). The Temple is an object made by human hands, and yet the Psalmist showed reverence to it to acknowledge God's presence with it. If the Jews could rightly reverence or venerate the temple of God, then why couldn't we rightly reverence or venerate the saints' images to signify our reverence of them who are mini-temples of God, having God's life dwelling within them? The answer is, we can.

From acceptable acts of bowing in the Bible

The Bible is replete with examples where an act of bowing is seen as a legitimate act of veneration of a creature. For example, Solomon reverenced his mother, Bathsheba, when he bowed before her in 1 Kings 2:19. He wasn't worshiping her. It was a gesture of honor given her as queen mother.

Other examples of approved bowing that connotes reverence for a creature include the following:

- Joshua bows before an angel in Josh. 5:14.

- Ruth bows before Boaz in Ruth 2:8-10.

- The Shunamite woman bows before Elisha after he resurrects her child in 2 Kings 4:37.

- Lot bows before two angels in Genesis 19:1.

- David bows before Saul in 1 Samuel 24:8.

- Bathsheba and Nathan bow before David in 1 Kings 1:16 and 25.

- Jacob bows before Esau seven times in Genesis 33:3.

So the pious act of bowing can be a legitimate act of showing veneration for a creature. Since the Church teaches that such venerating acts before the images of saints are transferred

CH 6: IT'S GOOD TO VENERATE THEM WITH IMAGES

to their "prototype"—that's to say, the honor is transferred to the person whose image it is—it follows that the pious act of bowing before an image of a saint has some biblical precedent. And if that's the case, then a Christian is assured that it's legitimate to bow before an image of a saint as a visible sign of his reverence for the saint.

From the instruction of a holy kiss

Several times through Paul's writings, he exhorts Christians to greet each other with a "holy kiss"—possibly a kiss on the lips, but one that excluded all unchasteness and merely served as an expression of fraternal love.[114] For example, he tells the Christians in Rome: "Greet one another with a holy kiss. All the churches of Christ greet you" (Rom. 16:16). He gives this exhortation three other times throughout his writings: 1 Corinthians 16:20, 2 Corinthians 13:12, and 1 Thessalonians 5:12. Paul even receives a holy kiss from the clergy in Ephesus (Acts 20:37).

A "holy kiss," as described by Paul, is an act of veneration—that's to say, it's a way in which one shows reverence for the other. So, if Paul can exhort Christians to venerate each other here on earth with a holy kiss, then, surely, Christians can venerate the saints in heaven with a holy kiss of their image, especially since the kissing of the image is meant to be a visible expression of their veneration of the saint whom the image represents.

Now, a Protestant might counter and say that the kisses Paul encourages and receives are not acts of veneration.[115] There is no ritual involved here, and it's not practiced within the context of worship. Rather, such kisses are merely acts of "affection or respect."[116]

The problem with this counter is that it makes a distinction without a difference. As mentioned above, the term "veneration" comes from the Latin word *venerārī*, which can mean "to revere" or "to honor." Kissing someone with brotherly affection to show respect *is* an act of reverence or honor. It shows that you revere or honor your spiritual brother with an esteem such that he is worthy of your affection. So it does no good to counter our argument from the holy kiss by saying it's not an act of veneration, but merely a sign of affection or respect.

Arguments Against

Like with the arguments in favor, arguments against the veneration of religious images, and in particular images of the saints, can be divided into two categories: arguments against *having* religious images and arguments against the *veneration* of such images. Note that these arguments can be employed to attack the veneration of religious images in general *or* the images of the saints specifically. Most of these opposing arguments are biblical. However, some are historical in nature and even pertain to practical concerns.

Arguments Against *Having* Images of the Saints

God forbids having graven images.

God commands in Exodus 20:4-5,

> You shall not make for yourself a graven image, or any
> likeness of anything that is in heaven above, or that is

in the earth beneath, or that is in the water under the earth; you shall not bow down to them or serve them; for I the Lord your God am a jealous God.

God says, "No graven images," yet the Catholic Church has images all over the place, including images of the saints in heaven. Many argue that this Catholic practice contradicts God's word.[117]

The first thing we can say in response is that God can't be condemning the making of religious images in an absolute sense because we've already seen above biblical examples where God sanctions and blesses the making of religious images.[118]

But even with this in place, the question arises: "What was God condemning?" The commandment not to make graven images forbids the making of *idols*. Although English translations often use terms like "graven image" in this passage, the word used in Hebrew—*pesel*—refers to a specific *kind* of image: an idol.

The context bears this out. Consider the prohibition that precedes the making of "graven images" in verse 3: "You shall have no other gods before me." Then, after the passage in question, we read, "You shall not bow down to them or *serve* them; for I the Lord your God am a jealous God." Given this contextual prohibition of idolatry, it's reasonable to conclude that God's command not to make "graven images" refers to making images to be worshiped as deities or idols.

Furthermore, every time the Hebrew word for "graven images" (*pesel*) is used in the Old Testament, it's used in reference to *idols* or the *images of idols*. For example, the prophet Isaiah warns in 44:9, "All who make idols [*pesel*] are nothing,

147

and the things they delight in do not profit; their witnesses neither see nor know, that they may be put to shame."*

Since making idols is what this commandment forbids, the Catholic custom of using statues and images for religious purposes doesn't contradict it, because Catholics don't use them as idols. Paragraph 2132 in the *Catechism* states the following:

> The Christian veneration of images is not contrary to the first commandment, which proscribes idols. Indeed, "the honor rendered to an image passes to its prototype," and "whoever venerates an image venerates the person portrayed in it." The honor paid to sacred images is a "respectful veneration," not the adoration due to God alone.

Catholics don't treat statues or the saints whom the statues represent as gods. As such, the biblical prohibition of idolatry doesn't apply.

This challenge from modern Evangelicals shows that there's nothing new under the sun. As mentioned above, the Catholic Church dealt with this sort of objection all the way back in the eighth century, when it condemned the heresy of *iconoclasm* at the Second Council of Nicaea (787).

In having images or statues of Jesus, angels, Mary, and the saints in its places of worship, the Catholic Church is following the Old Testament precedent of incorporating images of heavenly inhabitants that serve as reminders of who is present with us when we approach God in liturgical worship.

---

*   Other examples include but are not limited to Isa. 40:19, 45:20; Jer. 10:14, 51:17; and Hab. 2:18.

The representations of the cherubim in the Old Testament served as reminders that they are heavenly inhabitants present with God. Since humans have been admitted into heaven according to Revelation 5:8, 6:9, and 7:14–17, it's reasonable to employ representations of them, too.

King Hezekiah destroys the bronze serpent.

Some Protestants argue against having religious images and images of the saints by appealing to the destruction of the bronze serpent by King Hezekiah in 2 Kings 18:4. Gavin Ortlund is one such Protestant. In his online video, "Venerating Icons: A Protestant Critique," Ortlund argues as follows:

> The biggest problem is [that the bronze serpent] was destroyed by Hezekiah, and he's praised for destroying it precisely because it had become a snare to his people [2 Kings 18:4]. . . . Israel had made offerings to it. So, you know, this is a great example of what Protestants think happened: something good happens, and then people start to idolize it in various ways, and Hezekiah is praised for destroying it.

Our response to this argument is like our response in chapter four to Ortlund's argument against the practice of invoking the saints. Notice here that Ortlund rejects having religious images *because* in some instances, having a religious image led to a violation of God's law.

But, as we argued in chapter four, why should we reject having religious images, and in particular images of the saints, simply because *some* instances of having such images crossed the line and *led to* a violation of God's law? To repeat, we don't reject interpreting Scripture just because some interpretations lead people to their destruction (see 2 Pet. 3:15-16). Nor do we reject the practice of religion simply because some who practice it do so in a way that leads to unjust conflict and violence.

In a case where a religious image or an image of a saint is *worshiped*, the problem wouldn't be with the possession of such images. Rather, the problem would be with the specific intent to worship that's associated with having such images, like in the case when the Israelites began to venerate the bronze serpent with the intent to worship it *as a deity*.

Now, if that's the case, there's no need for Ortlund to persuade others away from the practice of honoring the saints by *having* their images. There could be some instances of having a religious image that doesn't involve a violation of God's law and thus is worthy of Christian practice.

Arguments Against *Venerating* Images of the Saints

God forbids bowing before religious images.

If a Protestant doesn't have a problem with *having* religious images, he most likely will have a problem with specific acts of veneration that we perform in front of such images, like bowing. For these Protestants, Catholics might *say* they don't worship the statues of saints, but their *actions* speak otherwise.

Exodus 20:5 is a go-to text for support.[119] After commanding that the Israelites shouldn't make "graven images," God says, "You shall not bow down to them or serve them." How can Catholics bow before images of saints, so it's argued, when the Bible explicitly forbids such activity?

In response, a question immediately arises: "Is God forbidding the act of bowing before images in and of itself? Or is he forbidding the act of bowing before a *specific kind* of image?"

The objection assumes the former. But such an assumption would be true if and only if an act of bowing before a creature were in and of itself an act of worship. As we've seen above, that's clearly not the case. The Bible is replete with examples of legitimate acts of bowing before creatures as a sign of veneration or reverence.

Moreover, Jesus himself says in Revelation 3:9 that he will make "those of the synagogue of Satan" "bow down" before the feet of the Christians in Philadelphia. If bowing before another were in and of itself an act of worship, then Jesus would be causing "those of the synagogue of Satan" to be guilty of idolatry. But that's absurd.

So God must be forbidding the act of bowing before a *specific kind* of image. What kind of image might that be? He's condemning the act of bowing before an *idol*. Recall from above that the "graven images" that God refers to are *idols*—as indicated by the Hebrew word *pesel*.

Since religious images, and in particular the images of saints, aren't idols, bowing in front of them doesn't *necessarily* take on the character of idol worship. The *intent* to worship the image with such an act would be necessary for it to count as worship. Consequently, the pious act of bowing in front of a saint's image, at least with the intention to give reverence to the represented saint that is due to a perfected *creature* of God, isn't an act prohibited by Exodus 20:5.

There's another possible response. The above argument envisions God's command as having a particular limit—namely, it prohibits the making of *idols*. But there's another possible limit that we could envision.[120]

In the Old Testament, God prohibited the Israelites from doing several things. For example, they weren't allowed to eat pork or drink blood. Now, such precepts are no longer binding for us as Christians today (see Col. 2:16). Why? The temptations that the precepts were meant to counter for the Israelites no longer exist.

Perhaps the prohibition against "graven images" was similar. Even if we consider for argument's sake that the precept extended to *all* religious images, it wouldn't necessarily follow that such images are prohibited today for Christians. The reason for the commandment was to help the Israelites avoid that which they were prone to: idolatry. God had to take extra measures to underscore for the Israelites the invisible nature of God in contrast to the pagan deities. Given that God's people have matured over time and are no longer prone to such sinful behavior with the advent of Christ and the grace that he gives, and given that Christ revealed that he is the visible image of the Father (John 14:9), there is no longer a need for the precept to forbid religious images.

So, like the kosher laws, it's possible that the prohibition of "images" could have been a temporary precept that was for a specific time and a specific purpose. And given that the achievement of such a purpose is no longer needed, the precept is no longer binding.

Regardless of which way we envision the commandment, it doesn't pose a threat to the Catholic practice of venerating the images of saints.

Now, there are a few counters that a Protestant might make to our above response. The first one appeals to instances in the Bible when a human being is reprimanded for bowing before another person, whether another human being or an angel. For example, in Acts 10:26, Cornelius bows down to adore Peter and is ordered to "stand up; I too am a man." Similarly, when John bows before an angel in Revelation 9:10, the angel reprimands him: "You must not do that! I am a fellow servant with you."

All these two passages show is that bowing can take on different meanings within different contexts. We showed above that there are circumstances where bowing is deemed appropriate. Apparently, the events involving Cornelius and John were circumstances where bowing was deemed inappropriate.

Therefore, the appeal to instances where bowing is inappropriate doesn't prove that bowing before a saint's image is wrong. It only cautions us to make sure our gesture of bowing is appropriate. The way to do that is to recognize that images, and the saints they represent, are not gods. If we do this, we're not worshiping them as gods and thereby not committing idolatry.

Another counter is that we're reading into Exodus 20:5 a distinction between acts of bowing that are not worship and acts of bowing that are worship.[121]

True, the text itself doesn't make this distinction. But the question shouldn't be whether the text makes such a distinction. Rather, it should be whether the distinction is legitimate.[122] And given the evidence from above that the Bible approves of bowing before creatures that aren't taken as idols, we can apply the distinction to Exodus 20:5 and conclude that God is condemning acts of bowing before images that are adoration in kind.

A third possible counter is that all the above bowing examples involve acts of bowing before *human beings*. Thus, it might be argued that the comparison between such instances of bowing and bowing before non-living objects, like an image of a saint or a statue, is disanalogous. Ortlund makes this argument in his video "Venerating Icons: A Protestant Critique." He states,

Now, this is not to say that the distinction between worship and veneration or other forms of respect has no validity in any context. When a knight bows down to a king, for example, this can be an act of homage, not an act of idolatry. Bowing down to people has a different range of meanings throughout different human cultures and it occurs in many places of the Bible. But that is disanalogous to an ongoing liturgical veneration directed to non-living objects....You find examples in Holy Scripture of people bowing down to other people. You never find examples of people bowing down to non-living objects in this liturgical act of reverence.

There are a few things to say in response. First, insofar as Ortlund acknowledges that a physical act of bowing can be legitimately used to show reverence for a person, he implicitly acknowledges that such an act can be legitimately employed to reverence a *creature*. Well, an image of a saint is a creature. Therefore, it's at least possible that a physical act of bowing could legitimately take on the significance of showing reverence for an image. If the intent is to show respect or reverence for the image *as a creature*, then, according to Ortlund's own logic, there would be nothing wrong with such an act.

Moreover, the reverence shown to the image of a saint by an act of bowing is intended to be transferred over to the person whose image it is anyway. Recall from above the Council of Trent's statement: "The honor that is shown [the image] is *referred to the prototypes* which those images represent."[123] Again, such an act would be consistent with Ortlund's logic.

One more thing. Ortlund seems to be hung up on the act of bowing as a form of "liturgical veneration." But why would a *liturgical* setting somehow change the nature of the act if the intent is to offer reverence due to a creature? If the *intent* is what determines the meaning of the bow *outside* the liturgy, then it's going to be the intent that determines the meaning of the bow *within* a liturgical setting. And if the intent of the bow is to reverence an image insofar as it represents a *creature* of God, which it should be, then Ortlund shouldn't have any problem with such a bow, even *within* liturgical settings.

Now, perhaps Ortlund wants to restrict his objection to there being no evidence in the Bible of people bowing before non-living objects. If that's the case, then we'd have to reply with the same lines of argumentation that we used in chapter four in response to Ortlund's objections that the Bible never instructs us to invoke the saints' intercession and his objection that the Bible has no instances of Christians practicing the invocation of the saints. There is no need to rehash those arguments here.

Acts of veneration are too close to adoration, and they make it easy for people to fall into idolatry.

Another concern Ortlund expresses is that acts of veneration look too much like worship and can lead people into idolatry. Here's his explanation:

> Okay, here's the ultimate Protestant concern in this. ...There's a naïveté about how idolatry can sneak in actual practice. Imagine a person who's bowing down before a statue of Mary outside of a church asking for forgiveness, or a woman who's lighting candles and kneeling before an icon of the apostle John nightly in her home. Is there any Christian anywhere in the first

500 years of Church history who would not conclude that is idolatry?

Externally, it looks the same. And internally, it's extremely hard to know when that line is crossed in the human heart. In the heart of a person engaging like this, is it not easy for feelings of loyalty and hope and affection and trust to sneak in, being given to this creature, that should only be given to the Creator, given the dire mentality of Scripture regarding idolatry? Why are such practices not more concerning for Protestants? This is just really strange to us.[124]

Ortlund's argument here is similar in structure to his argument against the invocation of Mary in the *Cursus Honorum*, which was addressed above. There, he expressed concern that invocations of Mary's intercession throughout Church history led to what he perceived to be distortions of the gospel. And because of such "distortions," so Ortlund concludes, Christians ought not to involve themselves in such a practice.

Here, concerning the veneration of images, he argues along the same lines. Since the act of bowing before images of saints might lead some people into the sin of idolatry, Christians ought to refrain from such practices.

Our responses to his concern with the invocation of Mary apply here as well. Assuming that some people actually do worship the images of saints, we shouldn't reject the veneration of saints' images on these grounds any more than we should reject the practice of interpreting Scripture on the grounds that some distort it. The abuse of a good practice doesn't negate the goodness of the practice itself.

> ### The early Church Fathers condemned the practice of venerating religious images.

Some Protestant apologists argue the early Church Fathers were obstinately opposed to the veneration of religious images.[125] They quote Fathers of the pre-Constantinian era (before 313) who seem to suggest that Christians considered the veneration of images an illegitimate practice. This being the case, it's concluded that the Catholic and Orthodox practice of venerating images of saints has departed from the apostolic faith.

The scope of this book doesn't allow me to consider *every* early Church Father cited to this end.[126] Consequently, I will cite only three here and offer my responses. The three cited, however, are representative of what many of the Fathers say concerning the veneration of images in the early Church.

Justin Martyr, a second-century Christian apologist, is often the first witness brought to bear on this issue.[127] In his *First Apology*, he writes,

> And neither do we honor with many sacrifices and garlands of flowers such deities as men have formed and set in shrines and called gods; since we see that these are soulless and dead, and have not the form of God (for we do not consider that God has such a form as some say that they imitate to his honor), but have the names and forms of those wicked demons that have appeared.
>
> For why need we tell you who already know, into what forms the craftsmen, carving and cutting, casting and hammering, fashion the materials? And often out of vessels of dishonor, by merely changing the form,

> and making an image of the requisite shape, they make what they call a god; which we consider not only senseless, but to be even insulting to God, who, having ineffable glory and form, thus gets his name attached to things that are corruptible, and require constant service.[128]

Like with the objection from Exodus 20:5, this appeal to Justin conflates the issue of *idolatry* with the practice of venerating religious images in and of itself. Justin is clear in the above passage that what's going on is *idolatry*: they offer "sacrifices" to "deities" and the images that men have formed and set in their shrines, which they call "gods." It's *idolatry* that Justin and Christians reject, not the veneration of religious images.

But what about the "garland of flowers"? Don't Catholics put flowers at the feet of a statue of Mary? Yes, they do. But flowers don't have an *inherent* meaning of adoration the way sacrifice does. The giving of flowers, therefore, can take on the meaning of due honor given to a creature.

Another point that's disanalogous to the Christian practice of venerating images is the pagan belief that the carved statues were alive, or at least had the deity dwelling within the images. This is indicated by Justin's insistence that the images of the deities were "soulless and dead." Christian veneration of images doesn't involve the belief that the images are alive, or that the saints they represent somehow inhabit the image. If someone were to believe this, he would be wrong and in need of correction.

Another second-century Christian apologist appealed to is Irenaeus. Concerning the followers of one named Carpocrates, Irenaeus writes the following in his *Against Heresies*:

They also possess images, some of them painted, and others formed from different kinds of material, while they maintain that a likeness of Christ was made by Pilate at that time when Jesus lived among them. They crown these images and set them up along with the images of the philosophers of the world; that is to say, with the images of Pythagoras, and Plato, and Aristotle, and the rest. They have also other modes of honoring these images, after the same manner of the Gentiles.[129]

There are several things we can say in response. First, it's ambiguous as to whether Irenaeus is condemning the veneration of images as such or if he's objecting to the veneration of the *Carpocratian* images, whatever they were. Perhaps the images they had were not something worthy of respect and being placed alongside the philosophers of the world. This suggestion is not outside the boundaries of plausibility, given that Hippolytus tells us the Carpocratians were in "the habit of invoking the aid of subordinate demons and dream-senders."[130] Perhaps the images were of these "demons" and "dream-senders."

Now, someone might counter that this response won't work because Hippolytus, in his *Refutation of All Heresies*, identifies these "images" as images of Christ created by Pilate. He writes, "They make counterfeit images of Christ, alleging that these were in existence at the time (during which our Lord was on earth, and that they were fashioned) by Pilate."

If this is the case, then such images would fall under the category of images that ought not to be venerated because Hippolytus says they're "counterfeit." On this reading, Irenaeus wouldn't be condemning the veneration of images of Christ. Rather, he'd be condemning the veneration of *counterfeit* images of Christ.

159

There's another plausible interpretation as to what Irenaeus is disapproving of on this reading.[131] Earlier in the chapter, Irenaeus lists the Carpocratians' denial of Christ's divinity among other problematic doctrines.[132] Combine this with their placement of Christ's images *alongside* the philosophers of the world. It may be that the Carpocratians' veneration of Christ's images was not at all different from how they venerated the images of the philosophers of the world, thereby indicating their belief that Christ was worthy of no more respect than these philosophers. A practice that signifies Christ being less than divine is definitely something subject to disapproval by Irenaeus.

There's another response to this objection from Irenaeus.[133] Notice that Justin makes clear that he's rejecting image veneration only of a particular kind—namely, "the same manner of the Gentiles." This leaves open the possibility that if image veneration were *not* after the manner of the Gentiles, then it could be something worthy of Christian practice.

Clement of Alexandria, a third-century theologian, is another early Father appealed to by Protestants for support of their rejection of the veneration of religious images. Although he doesn't say anything specifically about *acts* of veneration, he does seem to be against *having* religious images. And if that's the case, then, surely, he'd be against venerating such images.

Here's what he writes in his *Stromata*:

> Moses ages before enacted expressly, that neither a graven, nor molten, nor molded, nor painted likeness should be made; so that we may not cleave to things of sense, but pass to intellectual objects: for familiarity with the sight disparages the reverence of what is divine; and to worship that which is immaterial by matter, is to dishonor it by sense.[134]

Without its proper context, the above passage seems to express disfavor with "things of sense" and the worship of the immaterial "by matter" of *any* kind. But that's not what the context reveals.

Consider, for example, the sentence that comes immediately before the above passage: "'Don't wear a ring, nor engrave on it the images of *the gods*,' enjoins Pythagoras." The appeal to Moses' prohibition against graven images and disapproval of worshiping the immaterial by matter is Clement's argument against engraving rings with images of *pagan deities*. The rejection of *inappropriate* religious images doesn't entail a rejection of religious images *per se*.

Furthermore, in chapter five of book seven within the same work, Clement gives us an insight as to what the pagans with whom he's corresponding believed about these images. He writes,

> Is it not the case that rightly and truly we do not circumscribe in any place that which cannot be circumscribed; nor do we shut up in temples made with hands that which contains all things? . . .
>
> And what can be localized, there being nothing that is not localized? Since all things are in a place. And that which is localized having been formerly not localized, is localized by something. If, then, God is localized by men, he was once not localized, and did not exist at all.[135]

Given this context, it's clear that Clement is responding to pagans who worshiped the images of their pagan deities because they believed that their deities were "localized," or contained, within such images. This explains what Clement means when he says, "Familiarity with the sight disparages the reverence of what is divine; and to worship that which is immaterial by matter, is to dishonor it by sense." By "familiarity with the sight" and "worship by matter," Clement isn't referring to material images themselves. Rather, he's referring to the material images that the pagans thought their deities dwelt within. Of course, to think of divinity as being reducible to matter is to "disparage the reverence of what is divine." And any practice that suggests this ought to be rejected. But this is entirely disanalogous to the Catholic practice of the veneration of the saints' images. Therefore, it can't be used as evidence against it.

There is a lack of positive affirmation of the veneration of saints' images.

A Protestant may be willing to accept the above conclusion that the early Fathers weren't *condemning* the veneration of religious images in and of itself. However, he might argue that the early Fathers' statements, like the ones quoted above, indicate that image veneration wasn't a Christian practice.[136]

Notice that Justin, Irenaeus, and Clement never offer the Christian practice of image veneration as an alternative to what they're condemning. You'd think, so the argument might go, that if the early Christians were practicing image veneration, they would have offered their pagan correspondents the Christian practice as a replacement for the pagan idolatrous practices. Since they don't, it seems reasonable to conclude that image veneration wasn't a practice of the earliest days of Christianity. This being the case, we as Christians shouldn't engage in such a practice.

The first thing to note in response is that this objection takes the same form as the objection from chapter four concerning the lack of evidence from the first- and second-century Fathers for the *invocation* of the saints' intercession. Consequently, the answers given there apply here as well. As such, I will not rehash them. I recommend reading those answers with this objection in mind.

There is one answer, however, that applies specifically to this objection and is worth highlighting. Given that pagan culture of the first few centuries was steeped in idol worship, which involved the belief that their deities dwelt within the idols, it's possible that the early Christians shied away from offering the Christian practice of image veneration to keep their pagan correspondents from thinking that Christ and the saints dwell within their images. The pagans would have been prone to transfer their beliefs about idols over to Christian images.

So perhaps the absence of evidence of Christian image veneration in the first few centuries is not evidence for the absence of the practice after all. But, as we've said above, even if it is, that doesn't mean we ought to refrain from adopting the practice.

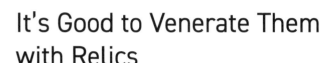

CHAPTER 7

It's Good to Venerate Them with Relics

I n our previous chapter, we dealt with the veneration of the saints' *images*. There's another way that Christians throughout the centuries have honored the saints, and that's through the veneration of their *relics*. Below we will look at favorable and unfavorable arguments for having and venerating relics.

Arguments in Favor

There are two kinds of arguments that we can make for the veneration of relics. The first is biblical in nature, which appeals to both the Old Testament and the New Testament. The second is historical, looking to extra-biblical Christian sources ranging from the second to the fourth century. We will consider our argument from the Bible first.

From the Bible

When it comes to honoring the saints with their relics, the Church simply follows Scripture. Perhaps the clearest example is 2 Kings 13:20-21, where we read about the bones of Elisha bringing a dead man back to life:

> Elisha died, and they buried him. Now bands of Moabites used to invade the land in the spring of the year. And as a man was being buried, lo, a marauding band was seen and the man was cast into the grave of Elisha; and as soon as the man touched the bones of Elisha, he revived, and stood on his feet.

In the New Testament, we have evidence that people sought out a few objects touched by St. Paul. For example, in Acts 19:11-12, St. Luke tells us, "God did extraordinary miracles by the hands of Paul, so that handkerchiefs or aprons were carried away from his body to the sick, and diseases left them and the evil spirits came out of them."

Luke also records that many believed that Peter's shadow could heal the sick (Acts 5:15). St. Matthew tells us that a hemorrhaging woman touched Jesus' garment and was healed (Matt. 9:20).

So the Catholic practice of having and venerating relics is at least *rooted* in Scripture.

From early Christian testimony

The first witness to the Christian practice of possessing and venerating saints' relics comes from the Epistle of the Church at Smyrna (c. A.D. 156), which concerns the martyrdom of

Polycarp, which happened in the early second century. The epistle reads,

> The centurion, seeing the strife excited by the Jews, placed [Polycarp's] body in the midst of the fire, and consumed it. Accordingly, we afterward took up his bones, as being more precious than the most exquisite jewels, and more purified than gold, and deposited them in a fitting place, whither, being gathered together, as opportunity is allowed us, with joy and rejoicing, the Lord shall grant us to celebrate the anniversary of his martyrdom, both in memory of those who have already finished their course, and for the exercising and preparation of those yet to walk in their steps.[137]

One thing to note here is that these Christians didn't collect the remains of Polycarp simply for the sake of remembrance. They performed *acts* of veneration. They *considered* them as "more precious than the most exquisite jewels...more purified than gold." They "*deposited* them in a fitting place," and they had the intention to "*celebrate* the anniversary of his martyrdom" with the relics. Although it doesn't speak of kissing or bowing, such acts are indeed acts of veneration.

St. John Chrysostom, bishop of the fourth century, provides a powerful witness to the possession and veneration of relics. In his Homily on St. Ignatius, he writes,

> Not the bodies only, but the very sepulchers of the saints have been filled with spiritual grace. For if in the case of Elisha this happened, and a corpse when it touched the sepulcher, burst the bands of death and

returned to life again, much rather now, when grace is more abundant, when the energy of the spirit is greater, is it possible that one touching a sepulcher, with faith, should win great power; thence on this account God allowed us the remains of the saints, wishing to lead by them us to the same emulation, and to afford us a kind of haven, and a secure consolation for the evils which are ever overtaking us.[138]

Note how John Chrysostom appeals to Elisha from the Old Testament. This represents the fourth-century belief that the Christian practice of having and venerating relics had biblical roots.

We also have evidence from St. Athanasius, the famous fourth-century bishop of Alexandria, concerning the "sheepskin" garments of Anthony of Padua. Athanasius first records Anthony's instructions given to his fellow monks concerning his garments:

> Divide my garments. To Athanasius the bishop, give one sheepskin and the garment whereon I am laid, which he himself gave me new, but which with me has grown old. To Serapion the bishop, give the other sheepskin, and keep the hair garment yourselves. For the rest fare ye well, my children, for Anthony is departing, and is with you no more.[139]

Athanasius then tells us what the monks did after Anthony died:

> He died and was gathered to the fathers. And they afterward, according to his commandment, wrapped him up and buried him, hiding his body underground.

And no one knows to this day where it was buried, save those two only. But each of those who received the sheepskin of the blessed Anthony and the garment worn by him guards it as a precious treasure. For even to look on them is as it were to behold Anthony; and he who is clothed in them seems with joy to bear his admonitions.

Similar to the Christians who reverenced the remains of Polycarp in the second century, the monks treated the garments of Anthony like "precious treasure" and "looked on them" with great devotion. Such acts might not be kissing and bowing, but they are nevertheless acts of veneration.

St. Basil of Caesarea is another witness to the Christian possession and veneration of relics. He speaks of relics in three of his letters. In Letter 49, he expresses to Bishop Arcadius his desire to *have* a relic of a martyr: "If I am able to find any relics of martyrs, I pray that I may take part in your earnest endeavor."[140]

In Letter 155, believed to be written to Julius Soranus (a relative of Basil), Basil affirms the good of *reserving relics in the home*: "If you send the relics of the martyrs home you will do well; as you write that the persecution there is, even now, causing martyrs to the Lord."[141]

Finally, in his 197th letter, a letter to Ambrose of Milan, Basil speaks of one named "Therasius the presbyter" and praises him for collecting and preserving relics with reverence. He writes,

Therasius the presbyter. He voluntarily undertook all the toil of the journey; he moderated the energy of the faithful on the spot; he persuaded opponents by his arguments; in the presence of priests and deacons, and of many others who fear the Lord, he took up the relics with all becoming reverence, and has aided the brethren in their preservation.[142]

To collect and preserve relics with reverence is an act of veneration. Basil then goes on to speak of how Ambrose received the relics with "joy":

> These relics do you receive with a joy equivalent to the distress with which their custodians have parted with them and sent them to you. Let none dispute; let none doubt. Here you have that unconquered athlete. These bones, which shared in the conflict with the blessed soul, are known to the Lord.

Again, there might not be any kissing or bowing going on, but Ambrose's joyful reception of these relics is an act of veneration.

There's one last witness we will look at here: St. Jerome. He takes on one named Vigilantius concerning a variety of issues, one of which is the veneration of relics. These are recorded in his work *Against Vigilantius*, which dates to around 406.

Let's begin with Jerome's statement of Vigilantius's charge:

> Among other blasphemies, he may be heard to say, "What need is there for you not only to pay such honor, not to say adoration, to the thing, whatever it may be, which you carry about in a little vessel and worship?" And again, in the same book, "Why do you kiss and adore a bit of powder wrapped up in a cloth?"[143]

Notice the charge of *kissing* the "bit of powder wrapped up in a cloth." Jerome confirms in his response below that such powder is a relic of martyrs. And he defends such veneration, writing,

> Tell us more clearly (that there may be no restraint on your blasphemy) what you mean by the phrase "a bit of powder wrapped up in a costly cloth in a tiny vessel." It is nothing less than the relics of the martyrs which he is vexed to see covered with a costly veil, and not bound up with rags or hair-cloth, or thrown on the midden, so that Vigilantius alone in his drunken slumber may be worshiped.

> Are we, therefore, guilty of sacrilege when we enter the basilicas of the apostles? Was the Emperor Constantius I guilty of sacrilege when he transferred the sacred relics of Andrew, Luke, and Timothy to Constantinople? In their presence the demons cry out, and the devils who dwell in Vigilantius confess that they feel the influence of the saints.

> And at the present day is the Emperor Arcadius guilty of sacrilege, who after so long a time has conveyed the bones of the blessed Samuel from Judea to Thrace? Are all the bishops to be considered not only sacrilegious, but silly into the bargain, because they carried that most worthless thing, dust and ashes, wrapped in silk in golden vessel? Are the people of all the churches fools, because they went to meet the sacred relics, and welcomed them with as much joy as if they beheld a living prophet in the midst of them, so that there was one great swarm of people from

Palestine to Chalcedon with one voice re-echoing the praises of Christ?[144]

Notice that Jerome justifies the reverence shown to relics by appealing to the *widespread practice*. In other words, this is not an isolated incident among only a few Christians.

Jerome finishes his defense by appealing to the miracles wrought through relics:

> I will not have you tell me that signs are for the unbelieving; but answer my question—how is it that poor worthless dust and ashes are associated with this wondrous power of signs and miracles?[145]

This is reminiscent of Paul's handkerchief healing the sick (Acts 19:11-12).

We could go on and on with more quotes from the Church Fathers, but the above quotes suffice to show that there is a strong early Christian testimony to the practice of the possession and veneration of relics.

Arguments Against

You can't jump from biblical examples of relics to the whole Catholic system of relics.

Some Protestants argue that the examples given above for relics in the Bible don't justify or lead to the Catholic practices surrounding relics. Here's Jordan Cooper's take:

There is no reason to say that [God's use of an ordinary object to bring about healing] somehow necessitates an entire system of the veneration of relics, where the Church owns relics and is able to dispense years off of purgatory for relics and the kind of superstition that arises around certain sacred objects that occurs throughout the Middle Ages.[146]

For Cooper, the "relic" examples in the Bible don't justify anything beyond recognizing that God can use physical objects to work miracles.

Gavin Ortlund makes the same argument but gives a specific *reason* why we can't jump from the biblical examples to the Catholic system. He argues,

In Holy Scripture there's really nothing exactly like a contemporary Catholic practice of relics. . . . [The biblical examples of relics are] different from people collecting the bones of Peter and Paul or anyone else after they're dead and thinking that there's some kind of veneration owed to them or help we may obtain from them. . . . What we see in the Bible and those kinds of examples with Peter's shadow and the handkerchiefs of Paul and the bones of Elisha just really are so different from a Catholic understanding of relics.[147]

The main problem for Ortlund here is that Catholic veneration of relics is just too different from the instances involving relics in the Bible. Due to such disparity, the Catholic practice can't be derived from these examples. The bottom line, at least for Ortlund, is that the Bible lacks examples of the type of veneration that Catholics give to relics.

To begin our response, let's take Cooper's formulation first. Under a "system of the veneration of relics," he lists three things: owning relics, dispensing years off purgatory with the use of relics, and superstition.

Concerning the alleged superstition and the dispensing of years off purgatory, these are alleged *abuses* associated with the use of relics. We will deal with this sort of objection a little later on below.

First, let's consider the Church's practice of collecting the remains of the saints and keeping them in safe keeping. Why wouldn't the relic examples from the Bible justify this? Luke tells us that Paul's handkerchief was being used to heal the sick. This implies that someone *had* the handkerchief in his possession and was making it available to be used.

Furthermore, the desire for and the actual pursuit of touching the handkerchief to heal illness is itself an act of veneration. That shows devotion to the relic itself. There's not much difference between that and the veneration of relics practiced today. So, at least when it comes to the example of Paul's handkerchief, we have biblical justification for viewing relics in a way that goes beyond simply recognizing that God can use physical objects to work miracles.

The veneration of relics has devolved into idolatrous and superstitious practices.

Another argument against the practice of venerating relics is its alleged devolution into idolatry and superstition. Concerning the superstition bit, Cooper argues,

> What we see is really an evolution of those ideas [about the general honor of saints] and a development

of those ideas in the medieval period to something that they were not intended to be initially. And that's when we get to the late medieval period[, where] we have so much superstition surrounding bones to saints…looking at them as it is a kind of magical object to some degree to give you special favors.[148]

Cooper also seems to think the practice has devolved into idolatry. He sees as problematic making a pilgrimage to the location where the relic is, kissing a relic, and bowing in front of it. But why would he think these are acts of inappropriate honor? The only explanation is that he thinks these are acts of honor due to God alone.

Ortlund concurs with Cooper in the idea that the practice of venerating relics has transgressed a boundary into the realm of superstition and idolatry. Here's Ortlund's argument:

The Protestant concern is that [of] idolatry and superstition in Church history. The use of relics develops and changes, and it gets to a point where it transgresses a boundary into the realm of—I'll use the words "superstition" and "idolatry"…adoring, kissing, embracing, and bowing to relics and in many cases venerating relics, thinking that this is a uniquely meritorious form of worship, making sacrifices unto relics as sacrifices unto God, thinking that the power or grace of God inheres in relics in such a way that if you draw near to the relic, or if you touch the relic, you can become a partaker of that grace or power.[149]

There are two approaches that we can take in answering this objection. The first is more general and is like what we've argued before: the abuse of a good practice doesn't negate the goodness of the practice itself. In earlier chapters, we used the example of interpreting Scripture. Peter tells us that some have done so to their own destruction (2 Pet. 3:15-16). But that doesn't mean we should get rid of the practice of interpreting Scripture.

Moreover, Paul's instructions concerning the gift of tongues in 1 Corinthians 14 suggest that some Christians in Corinth were abusing the gift. Must we avoid using the gift given because some have abused it? The logic of Cooper's and Ortlund's objection demands a "yes." But that's absurd, at least for a Christian who believes that the Holy Spirit still gives the gift of tongues today (such a Christian is called a *continuationist*[150]).

And even if such a gift were no longer given (a view known as *cessationism*), the logic would still demand that Christians in the first century avoid the use of the gift. But that's not Paul's instruction. Rather, he simply provides guidelines for appropriate use of the gift: "If any speak in a tongue, let there be only two or at most three, and each in turn; and let one interpret. But if there is no one to interpret, let each of them keep silence in church" (vv. 27-28).

Now, to be fair to Ortlund, he does acknowledge a legitimate respect that can be shown for relics and that relics can be used in the Christian life "for teaching and inspiration."[151] But it's the *forms* of respect listed above that are the real problem for Ortlund, since, as Ortlund expresses, they've "crossed a boundary."

This leads us to our second approach in response to Cooper's and Ortlund's argument: consider each of the acts of veneration that Cooper and Ortlund see as superstitious or idolatrous—for example, "making sacrifices unto relics as sacrifices unto God" and acts of veneration where the person thinks it's a "uniquely meritorious form of worship."

We agree that this would be idolatry, which "crosses a boundary and is no longer edifying and godly and something Jesus would want us to do." Anyone who has done this in the past, or currently does it in the present, or will do it in the future needs to repent and turn away from such idolatry. But, per our first approach, this isn't a reason to refrain from the practice of venerating relics.

Next comes bowing in front of relics and kissing them—but we already showed in a previous chapter that the acts of bowing and kissing are not idolatrous in and of themselves. Can they become idolatrous? Yes! But that's only because the person bowing or kissing does so with the intention to express an honor that belongs to God alone. If the bowing or kissing is done simply to express honor for the saint, who is worthy of it as a perfected creature of God, then it's not idolatry.

Now, when it comes to superstition, both Cooper and Ortlund see relic veneration as involving the belief that power resides in the relic itself. Cooper objects to "looking at [a relic] as…a kind of magical object to some degree to give you special favors." Ortlund sees a problem in "thinking that the power or grace of God inheres in relics in such a way that if you draw near to the relic, or if you touch the relic, you can become a partaker of that grace or power."

Cooper and Ortlund are right to reject these sorts of superstitious beliefs. In fact, they're thinking right in line with the Catholic Church. The *Catechism* sees "superstition" as a perversion of the virtue and practice of religion and defines it in the following way:

[Superstition is] when one attributes an importance in some way magical to certain practices otherwise lawful or necessary. To attribute the efficacy of prayers or of sacramental signs to their mere external performance, apart from the interior dispositions that they demand, is to fall into superstition (2111).

This definition of superstition would apply to the sort of beliefs surrounding relics that Cooper and Ortlund object to. To think that a certain power resides in the relics themselves and that we can tap into that power is superstitious. It's this superstition that the Council of Trent rejects in its statement on the veneration of relics: "[In the] veneration of relics...every superstition shall be removed."[152] Therefore, the perversion of relic veneration that Cooper and Ortlund reject is also rejected by the Catholic Church. No qualms here.

There are other items, however, that Ortlund lists as superstitious that we do have qualms with. Here's his list:

- thinking that a Eucharist celebration is more holy if it is celebrated on an altar that displays the relics of saints or martyrs

- thinking that prayer is more efficacious or more worthy if it is made near or while touching a relic

- that pilgrimages are highly to be valued to visit relics for the sake of having more meritorious prayers that God is more likely to answer

- indulgences for sin being given on the basis of touching or kissing or gazing upon a relic

- the belief that if you make an oath or a vow while touching a relic the sanctity of that oath or vow is directed to both God and the saints[153]

And then two more:

- hanging dirt from the holy land in a container to "ward off demons" and

- bringing the tooth of a martyr to a village to "protect a village from famine or from war."

Let's treat the first item listed above: the idea that having relics make the eucharistic celebration "more holy." If we are talking about the idea that the relic makes Mass itself more dignified in holiness, or makes the Mass have more power of itself, then we'd agree that this is an abuse. Nothing can make Jesus' body and blood, along with his offering of his body and blood to the Father, more perfect than what it already is.

But if by "more holy," we're considering that the relic can make the Mass have a greater effect *in us*, then we'd disagree that this is superstition. The effect that the Mass, or any prayer, has on us is dependent on our interior disposition for receiving the graces that Christ wills to communicate. Such a disposition can be affected in a positive way by the intercessory prayers of saints, whether directly via membership in the mystical body of Christ or via *impetration*, where they request that God grant us graces to properly dispose us. As St. James writes, "the prayer of a righteous man has great power in its effects" (James 5:16).

Now, although relics are not the saints themselves, they are signs of the saints' presence. And intentional veneration of the relics is a means by which we invoke the saints to be present by way of their intercession. So having a relic, whether at Mass or in a home, or pilgrimaging to the place of a revered relic, can indeed contribute to the effectiveness of prayers, especially the greatest prayer of the eucharistic celebration.

Moreover, the saints can help ward off evil through their intercessory prayer. Since having a relic is a way to invoke the saints' intercession, it follows that having their relics can ward off evil.

Here's another way to look at this issue. If God can use relics to bring about miraculous effects (as evidenced in the Bible with the bones of Elisha and Paul's handkerchief), then, surely, he can use relics to bring about spiritual goods, such as the fruits of our prayers and protection from evil.

But what about indulgences? It's hard to tell exactly what the problem is. Ortlund appeals to indulgences as an example of superstition. But if he thinks that temporal punishment due for a past *forgiven* sin is remitted (that's what an indulgence is) in virtue of some inherent power within the relic, then the charge doesn't stick, since the Catholic Church doesn't teach that relics have inherent power to remit temporal punishment due for sin.

If, however, the problem here is the Church's claim to remit temporal punishment due for sin on account of some act of reverence shown to a saint, then the problem is not with relics, but with the doctrine of indulgences, thereby shifting the conversation from relic veneration to indulgences, which is a topic that goes beyond the scope of this book.

Ortlund also brings up the practice of touching relics while professing vows. He views such a practice as superstitious. But, again, at least for Catholics, we don't believe that the relic itself has power to make the vow binding. That *would* be superstitious. Rather, touching the relic is simply a visible expression of what's primarily interior: the will to keep a promise, whether to

God or to a saint. This is no more problematic than raising your right hand with your left hand on a Bible when you formally swear to tell the truth in a court of law. Bodily gestures have meaning. And we should welcome such gestures, given that we're *human* beings.

There's one more problem that Ortlund raises: "people paying enormous sums of money to touch a relic so they can pray for their sick child." We Catholics are with Ortlund on this one. This *is* an abuse, and it was rectified at the Fourth Lateran Council (1215), way before the reforms issued by the twenty-fifth session of the Council of Trent (1563). Fourth Lateran declared,

> The Christian religion is frequently disparaged because certain people put saints' relics up for sale and display them indiscriminately. In order that it may not be disparaged in the future, we ordain by this present decree that henceforth ancient relics shall not be displayed outside a reliquary or be put up for sale. As for newly discovered relics, let no one presume to venerate them publicly unless they have previously been approved by the authority of the Roman pontiff.[154]

We acknowledge there were, are, and will be abuses surrounding the veneration of relics. But as above, abuses are not a justification for rejecting the practice wholesale.

The early Church's reverence of relics didn't take the form of those popular during medieval and current times.

Ortlund articulates another problem that he has with the medieval and current forms of relic veneration: it's a development from the reverence given by Christians in the early Church. What sorts of things does he have in mind? Pilgrimages, paying sums of money to touch the relics, thinking prayers will be more efficacious from touching the relics, etc.

Now, we've already said above that paying sums of money is an abuse. But we also argued that the other practices are legit when done with proper motives. So the question for Ortlund is, "Why can't we accept these practices as a *legitimate* development of relic veneration?"

The problem can't be the practices themselves, because we've already shown that they're legit. The only other option is that developments themselves are the problem, the assumed principle being that we can adopt only Christian practices that were present in the earliest centuries of the Church.

But we've already given answers to this sort of objection in previous chapters. (See the objection in chapter four concerning the lack of evidence from first- and second-century Fathers for the *invocation* of the saints' intercession along with the objection in chapter six concerning a lack of positive affirmation of the veneration of saints' images.) Therefore, Ortlund's criticism doesn't stick.

We're left, however, with an interesting question: "Why aren't elaborate forms of veneration found in the earliest centuries of the Church? Why didn't they come about until later in the fourth century?"

One plausible answer is that within the Roman Empire prior to Constantine, taking bodies, or parts of bodies, from graves was punishable by death.[155] The quote below comes from a first-century marble tablet found in Nazareth with a statement issued by the Roman emperor:

Edict of Caesar. It is my decision [concerning] graves and tombs—whoever has made them for the religious observances of parents, or children, or household members—that these remain undisturbed forever.

But if anyone legally charges that another person has destroyed, or has in any manner extracted those who have been buried, or has moved with wicked intent those who have been buried to other places, committing a crime against them, or has moved sepulcher-sealing stones, against such a person I order that a judicial tribunal be created, just as [is done] concerning the gods in human religious observances, even more so will it be obligatory to treat with honor those who have been entombed. You are absolutely not to allow anyone to move [those who have been entombed]. But if [someone does], I wish that [violator] to suffer capital punishment under the title of tomb-breaker.[156]

Given this rule, it's understandable why Christians wouldn't be digging up the remains of martyrs and saints and engaging in forms of veneration common in the medieval and current times. Consequently, they would be able to venerate relics only by visiting the sites and offering memorials at their tombs.

This would all change, however, in the fourth century. Charles Freeman, English historian of ancient Greece and Rome, notes,

With the granting of toleration to Christians by the emperor Constantine in A.D. 313, the bodies of martyrs from the second- and third-century persecutions of Christians could be brought out into the open, and it became the custom to place them in the central altar of the new basilicas. A verse from the Book of Revelation (6:9)—"I saw under the altar the souls of them that were slain for the word of God and the testimony which they held"—endorsed the practice, thus providing an effective link between Scripture and the veneration of Christian martyrs.[157]

When the threat of death no longer looms, it makes sense for Christians to begin venerating the remains of martyrs and saints in ways they couldn't do before. Hence the development of the veneration of relics.

Relics have too high of a propensity to lead people into superstition and idolatry.

There's one last concern that Ortlund expresses, which he identifies as the underlying impulse of the Protestant concern—namely, relic veneration has a "high propensity to become superstitious," and "the human heart does tend toward idolatry" and "tends to veer off track instead of seeking what we need from God himself."[158] In other words, for Ortlund, man is too weak to appropriate healthy relic veneration. The implied conclusion is that we ought to reject the developed practices of relic veneration within the Catholic Church (and the Orthodox churches, too).

We're right back in the same boat as before. What is precisely the problem? Is it the *propensity* to idolatry? Or is it the practices themselves that Ortlund perceives to be idolatrous?

If it's man's weakness and propensity to idolatry that is the problem, then we'd have to give up other things in the Christian life. For example, fallen man has a tendency to turn the pursuit of holiness into an evil pursuit of self-righteousness. Does this mean man ought not to pursue holiness? Of course not. The pursuit of holiness is a good thing.

If, however, the problem is the developed acts of veneration themselves, then there's no need to belabor the point, since we've already addressed this issue above. All the acts of veneration that Ortlund lists, besides the payment of money and sacrifices offered to relics, are not in themselves superstitious or idolatrous.

So, like Ortlund's other arguments, this one doesn't succeed in justifying the rejection of medieval and current forms of relic veneration.

CHAPTER 8

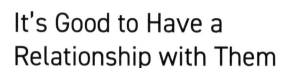

It's Good to Have a Relationship with Them

A pologetical arguments are necessary for discerning whether the practices of the invocation and veneration of the saints are good and holy. But such apologetical reflections are also necessary to move forward in establishing *relationships* with the saints. We can't foster loving relationships with and devotion to the saints if we don't first believe that the invocation and veneration involved in such a relationship are right and good.

Now, in moving forward with establishing such relationships, several questions remain: "Are patron saints part of the Christian life?" "What sort of approach should I take to a saint's writings when I'm trying to get to know a saint?" "Must I even have a devotion to a saint?" "Should I have a relationship with just one saint or many?"

It's these sorts of questions that we will address in this chapter.

Making Patron Saints Part of the Christian Life

A patron saint is a saint who's chosen as a special advocate for a particular area of life, whether it be an occupation, an illness, a church, a country, or some task—basically, anything that's important to us. This pious practice has its origins in the building of the first public churches in the Roman Empire, when Constantine decriminalized the practice of Christianity, many of which were built over the graves of martyrs. These churches were given the names of the martyrs over whose graves they were built, and it was piously believed that the martyr would pray in a special way for the Christians who worshiped there. Examples of these include St. Peter's Basilica, St. Paul Outside the Walls, St. Lawrence in Agro Verano, St. Sebastian, and St. Agnes on the Via Nomentana.

Over time, Christians would begin dedicating newly erected churches to other men and women believed to be in heaven but who were not martyrs, because that person was known for performing miracles, having high levels of holiness, or preaching the gospel in that area. The *Catholic Encyclopedia* explains that eventually, patronages would extend to "the ordinary interests of life, [a person's] health, and family, trade, maladies, and perils, his death, his city, and country." It further notes that "the whole social life of the Catholic world before the Reformation was animated with the idea of protection from the citizens of heaven."[159]

In recent centuries, the Holy See has announced several patrons. For example, on December 8, 1870, Pope Pius IX declared St. Joseph the patron of the universal Church. Pope Leo XIII announced several patrons during his pontificate. Just to name two, for example, he proclaimed St. Thomas Aquinas the patron of all universities, colleges, and schools and St. Vincent as the patron of all charitable societies.

These patronages normally were chosen due to the occupations, skills, or interests that these saints had while on earth. Also, saints who suffered from some malady or cared for people who did are often chosen as the patron for those who suffer from the same malady or their caregivers.

This pious practice has some basis in Scripture, which holds various figures up to us as examples. St. Paul, for instance, used Abraham as the example *par excellence* of faith and explained how imitation of Abraham's faith is necessary to be justified.

St. James instructs his readers to look to steadfastness of the prophets—namely, Job—as an example of suffering and patience. He writes in 5:10-11, "As an example of suffering and patience, brethren, take the prophets who spoke in the name of the Lord. Behold, we call those happy who were steadfast. You have heard of the steadfastness of Job, and you have seen the purpose of the Lord, how the Lord is compassionate and merciful." Recognizing that saints had experiences like ours during their lives, it became natural for Christians to look to their example, seek their intercession, and turn to them as patrons of these experiences.

There aren't too many early references in the early Church Fathers, but there are a couple that are worth sharing. The first is from St. Irenaeus. In book five, chapter nineteen of his *Against Heresies*, he speaks of Mary as the "patroness" or "advocate" of Eve. He writes,

> [Eve] did disobey God, yet [Mary] was persuaded to be obedient to God, in order that the Virgin Mary might become the patroness [Latin, *advocata*] of the virgin Eve.[160]

189

Exactly what Irenaeus means here is not entirely clear. But at least there is some sense in which Irenaeus sees the Blessed Virgin as having some special relationship with Eve.

The other reference is from St. Methodius of Olympus, who in 305, before Constantine came to power, wrote a prayer to St. Simeon, asking him for special intercession. Here's an excerpt from the prayer:

> O honored and venerable Simeon, you earliest host of our holy religion, and teacher of the resurrection of the faithful, be our patron and advocate with that Savior God, whom you were deemed worthy to receive into your arms.[161]

Establishing deep relationships with the saints in heaven is a good thing for us to do as Catholics. They are our brothers and sisters in the mystical body of Christ. Having patrons is a way to foster and deepen those relationships. Therefore, patron saints are a good part of our spiritual life as Catholics.

Getting to Know Saints Through Their Writings

Half of this book has been devoted to defending the honor or veneration that we give to the saints in heaven, both generally and in specific acts of veneration. But one might ask if such veneration includes believing what a saint says in his writings or private revelations.

Let's first consider what saints say in their ordinary writings. We can classify them into two categories: *Church-confirmed* and *non-Church-confirmed*.

Church-confirmed writings are distinguished by the level of authority they're given. Hypothetically, if a passage from the saint's writing is used in the context of a doctrinal definition, then it could be elevated to the level of infallibility, which would require from Catholics either what theologians call "divine and Catholic faith" or "firm and definitive assent," depending on whether the writing is used to define something that is part of divine revelation or intrinsically connected to it.

If a passage from the writing is used in the context of a teaching of the Ordinary Magisterium, it could, in the same way, itself be elevated to the level of a teaching of the Ordinary Magisterium. This sort of teaching would not require "divine and Catholic faith," nor "firm and definitive assent," but religious submission of intellect and will (see *Lumen Gentium* 25).

If a passage from the saint's writing is mentioned in a magisterial document, but not intrinsically connected to a particular doctrinal teaching, then it would be elevated to the level of an accepted Catholic opinion. We generally would say that such a teaching can be safely held by a Catholic.

For example, when the Church declared St. Thérèse of Lisieux a Doctor of the Church[162] because of her Little Way, it indicated that her Little Way is a safe form of spirituality for Catholics to pursue. The book in which she laid out the Little Way, *Story of a Soul*, can be treated as a helpful guide to the spiritual life. But there's no obligation for a Catholic to follow the Little Way in his own spiritual life. He just can't say it's "not Catholic."

There are also cases where the Church approves of a saint's writings, but such writings contain a particular teaching that a Catholic either *must* reject due to later infallible teaching or is *permitted* to reject due to the nature of the teaching or later developments in human knowledge. For example, the Church looks to the writings of St. Thomas Aquinas as a model for theology and philosophy.[163] But Catholics must reject his treatment of the Immaculate Conception (see *ST* III 27:2) to the extent that it conflicts with the Church's infallible declaration on that matter under Pope Pius IX in 1854 (see *Ineffabilis Deus*).[164]

We would *not* be obliged to reject Aquinas's view that angels move the celestial spheres.[165] This is not something the Church has made any pronouncement on. So a Catholic can either agree with Aquinas or part ways with him on this matter.

For writings by saints that are not Church-confirmed, there's no obligation to accept what they say (unless the Church has infallibly taught what the saint teaches independent of the saint's writing). This includes a pope's mention of a saint's writing in a non-magisterial context, such as in a private lecture or book.

Concerning private revelations, meaning those recognized by the authority of the Church, the Church simply affirms their authenticity and says they are *worthy* of belief, but not that they *must* be believed. As the *Catechism* states in paragraph 67, private revelations "do not belong . . . to the deposit of faith."

The deposit of faith, according to paragraph 84 in the *Catechism*, refers to the public revelation given to us by Christ and the apostles "contained in Sacred Scripture and Tradition." Such revelation demands faith because, in the words of the Dicastery for the Doctrine of the Faith in its document *The Message of Fátima*, in public revelation, "God himself speaks to us through human words and the mediation of the living community of the Church."[166]

Private revelations, on the other hand, according to that same document from the DDF, are "visions and revelations which have taken place since the completion of the New Testament," which are not meant to, as the United States Conference of Catholic Bishops puts it, "improve or complete Christ's definitive revelation, but to help live more fully by it in a certain period of history."[167]

Private revelations, therefore, are "in service to the faith" and show their credibility by "leading [us] back to the definitive public revelation." Since private revelations aren't part of definitive revelation, they do not require faith.

Joseph Cardinal Ratzinger, as prefect for the Dicastery (then Congregation) for the Doctrine of the Faith, confirmed this view in his theological commentary in *The Message of Fátima*. Ratzinger quotes Prospero Cardinal Lambertini, who became Pope Benedict XIV, concerning the type of assent a Catholic is to give and not give to private revelations:

> An assent of Catholic faith is not due to revelations approved in this way; it is not even possible. These revelations seek rather an assent of human faith in keeping with the requirements of prudence, which puts them before us as probable and credible to piety.

Ratzinger explains the reason for this difference in assent:

> The authority of private revelations is essentially different from that of the definitive public revelation. The latter demands faith; in it in fact God himself speaks to us through human words and the mediation of the living community of the Church. Faith in God and in his word is different from any other human faith, trust, or opinion. The certainty that it is God who is speaking gives me the assurance that I am in touch with truth itself. It gives me a certitude which is beyond verification by any human way of knowing.

The only persons for whom private revelations may be binding are the persons who receive them. In practice, we must look to the Magisterium of the Church, which, as the *Catechism* states in paragraph 67, "discerns and welcomes in these revelations whatever constitutes an authentic call of Christ or his saints to the Church."

Establishing a Devotion to the Saints

Another question that arises when we're talking about our relationship with the saints, and the honor that is due to them, is, "Must I have a devotion to the saints?"

Well, it depends on what we mean by devotion. If we intend to include within our definition of "devotion" the recognition of certain facts about them, then yes. For example, we must honor them by acknowledging their saintly status and our communion with them in the body of Christ. And, as mentioned in a previous chapter, given their status as members in the body of Christ, we must acknowledge their help: "There are many parts, yet one body. The eye cannot say to the hand, 'I have no need of you,' nor again the head to the feet, 'I have no need of you'" (1 Cor. 12:20-21). This includes recognizing that they intercede for us in heaven. Also, as the *Catechism* teaches in Paragraph 957, we must "cherish the memory of those in heaven," since it's a "fraternal exercise of charity" that strengthens the union of the Church.

Now, if what we mean by "devotion" is simply having an *emotional attachment* to the saints, then such "devotion" is not necessary. Unlike the devotion described above that simply requires assent, emotions are not something we can have direct and immediate control over. As such, emotional attachment to the saints is not something that can be required of us.

With that said, devotion in this sense is natural and can be developed just as emotional attachment to any person can be developed. And to develop such emotional attachments to our spiritual brothers and sisters in Christ would be a pious action for a Catholic.

So how do we develop such devotion?

One way is to learn more about the saints through reading apologetic and devotional literature. Apologetic literature seeks to articulate what the Church teaches about the saints and why. This provides a basis for properly relating to the saints in our devotional practices. We don't want to relate to the saints in ways that contravene what God has revealed to us.

Another way to foster a relationship with the saints is to have normal conversations with them as you would with a friend. You can't have a friendship with someone unless you talk to him. The saints are our friends, and as we've seen in Revelation 5:8, they are aware of what we're saying to them.

Other devotional practices include celebrating a saint's feast day, wearing a holy medal of the saint, or praying novenas in his honor. Take feast days, for example. In the *Roman Martyrology*, every day on the liturgical calendar honors a particular saint, and often multiple saints. Since these are days of celebration, we can foster devotion to a saint on his feast day by doing celebratory things: go to the Mass that commemorates the saint, put up a picture of the saint in a prominent place in the home, read something about the saint's life, or even just have an ice cream outing in his honor.

Holy medals of saints serve as a reminder of their heroic lives in Christ, urging us on to imitate them. Also, by wearing a medal of a saint, we're reminded to call upon him for help.

With regard to novenas, a simple search online provides a plethora of novena prayers. Whereas a novena involves a set

of nine prayers, similar devotions include the Six Sundays of
Aloysius, which was established in the eighteenth century by
Pope Clement XII to foster devotion to the youthful saint.[168]
Other devotions include the Five Sundays of Francis's Stigmata,
the Seven Sundays of the Immaculate Conception, the Seven
Sundays of St. Joseph, the Ten Sundays of St. Francis Xavier, and
the Ten Sundays of St. Ignatius Loyola.

St. Paul teaches us that the Church is the "household of
God" (1 Tim. 3:15). The saints in heaven are members of that
household. As such, it's important that we get to know our
fellow family members and foster love among the family.

Establishing a Relationship with a Variety of Saints

The last issue pertaining to our relationship with the saints,
and the last one that we're going to consider in this chapter, is
the good of having a relationship with a variety of saints.

St. Thomas Aquinas writes about this in the supplement to
his *Summa Theologiae*. But he does so as a response to an objection that he poses to himself. The objection is interesting to
consider. He states it this way:

> If we ought to beseech them to pray for us, this is
> only because we know their prayer to be acceptable
> to God. Now among the saints the holier a man is,
> the more is his prayer acceptable to God. Therefore
> we ought always to bespeak the greater saints to inter-
> cede for us with God, and never the lesser ones (*ST
> Suppl.* 72:2, ad 2).

Aquinas responds with five reasons why it's fitting, or good, to develop a devotion to even the lesser saints. First, we might connect better with a lesser saint, and thus have a greater or more intense devotion than we would have had with a greater saint. This is important because, as Aquinas teaches, "the effect of prayer depends very much on one's devotion" (*ibid.*).

Second, it's important that we not grow weary in our devotion and keep its fervor strong. This can be achieved by praying to different saints. The bottom line is, developing devotions to different saints keeps things fresh.

Third, related to what we talked about in our previous lesson, the saints exercise their patronage in special cases. I might need St. Joseph's help to be a good husband and father, but I need St. Thomas Aquinas to help me be a good apologist. Hence the need to develop a devotion to both saints, even though Aquinas is not given as much honor as given to St. Joseph.

Fourth, it's due to *all* the saints that we give them honor. Developing devotions to different saints, even the "lesser" ones, is a way in which we can give that honor due.

Finally, *the more the merrier*. As Aquinas writes, "the prayers of several sometimes obtain that which would not have been obtained by the prayers of one."

For these reasons, it's a good thing for us to develop devotions with a variety of our brothers and sisters in heaven.

Conclusion

In this book, we've looked at several things that pertain to the Catholic teaching on the saints. We learned what it means to be a saint and the variety of ways in which we can understand this: being a baptized Christian, a soul in heaven, or canonized.

In answering the several objections that our Protestant friends pose to us as Catholics, we learned that asking the saints to intercede for us doesn't take away from Christ, and it doesn't violate the Bible's prohibition of necromancy, nor does it make gods out of them.

We also saw how Protestants fail in their objections to show that asking the saints to pray for us is futile. The saints in heaven *do* know what's going on here on earth, they *are* aware of the requests we make of them, and they're able to do so because God communicates that information to them.

Moreover, contrary to what our Protestant friends think, there *is* biblical evidence that the saints in heaven intercede for us. Revelation 5:8 is very clear on this matter, as we've seen. And if that's what the saints are doing up in heaven, then it's reasonable for us to make our request known to them.

Finally, we saw that the Catholic practice of honoring or venerating the saints in no way contradicts what the Bible says. The pious act of bowing in front of statues that represent the saints is simply a form of honor that's essentially different from the honor we give to God. The pious devotion of keeping their relics is not superstition but another way of honoring our heroes in faith.

As I mentioned in our introduction, my hope is that having read this book, you better appreciate the union we have with the saints in heaven and enjoy more fully the family blessings, knowing that we have a host of heavenly allies cheering us on *and helping us* run the race of salvation. They are our brothers and sisters. Together, we are the "household of God" (1 Tim. 3:15). Let's not exclude ourselves from experiencing the fullness of blessings that come with the familial relationships within this household, including relationships with the saints in heaven.

About the Author

Karlo Broussard, DPhil., a native of Southern Louisiana, left a promising musical career to devote himself full-time to the work of Catholic apologetics. As a staff apologist and speaker for Catholic Answers, and a member of the chancery evangelization team at the Diocese of Tulsa and Eastern Oklahoma, he travels the country and the diocese giving talks on apologetics, biblical studies, theology, and philosophy. Karlo is a regular guest on *Catholic Answers Live* and contributor to *Catholic Answers Magazine* in its print and online editions.

Karlo holds a doctorate in philosophy from the Pontifical University St. Patrick's in Maynooth, Ireland, as well as undergraduate and graduate degrees in theology from Catholic Distance University and the Augustine Institute, and a master's in philosophy from Holy Apostles College and Seminary.

A dynamic and gifted Catholic speaker and author, Karlo is known for communicating with precision of thought, a genuine love for God, and an enthusiasm that inspires.

Endnotes

1   Research for these Bible passages is taken from Jimmy Akin, *A Daily Defense: 365 Days (Plus One) to Becoming a Better Apologist* (El Cajon, CA: Catholic Answers Press, 2016), 130.

2   *Catechism of the Catholic Church*, 2nd ed. (Libreria Editrice Vaticana, 1997).

3   United States Conference of Catholic Bishops, "Saints," http://www.usccb.org/about/public-affairs/backgrounders/saints-backgrounder.cfm.

4   Ibid.

5   Dicastery for the Doctrine of the Faith, "Doctrinal Commentary on concluding formula of 'Professio fidei,'" https://www.ewtn.com/catholicism/library/doctrinal-commentary-on-concluding-formula-of-professio-fidei-2038, emphasis added.

6   See Pope Paul VI, Motu Propio on Liturgical Year and New Universal Roman Calendar *Mysterii Paschalis* (Feb. 14, 1969), https://www.catholicculture.org/culture/library/view.cfm?id=5934.

7   Second Vatican Council, Pastoral Constitution on the Church in the Modern World *Gaudium Et Spes*, 22, www.vatican.va.

8   Council of Trent, Session 25, Dec. 4, 1563, "On the Invocation, Veneration, and Relics, of Saints, and on Sacred Images," in *The Canons and Decrees of the Sacred and Ecumenical Council of Trent*, ed. and trans. J. Waterworth (London: Dolman, 1848), 233, emphasis added.

9   Pope Benedict XII, Apostolic Constitution *Benedictus Deus*, https://www.papalencyclicals.net/ben12/b12bdeus.htm.

10   Unless otherwise noted, all quotations of Aquinas's works are taken from his corpus hosted at www.isidore.co.

11   For a treatment of what is required for a departed soul to have knowledge in the afterlife without its body—namely, a divine light (or grace)—see Aquinas, *Summa Theologiae* I:89:1, 4, 7, 8. See also Melissa Eitenmiller, "On the Separated Soul According to St. Thomas Aquinas," *Nova et Vetera* 17, no. 1 (2019):57-91; Edward Feser, "Some Questions on the Soul, Part II," Oct. 14, 2013, http://edwardfeser.blogspot.com/2013/10/some-questions-on-soul-part-ii.html; John F. Wippel, *Metaphysical Themes Vol. III* (Washington, D.C.: The Catholic University of America Press, 2021), ch. 7.

12   I am grateful to Jimmy Akin for sharing this research with me in conversation.

13   Council of Vienne, "De Summa Trinitate et Fide Catholica," in *The Sources of Catholic Dogma*, eds. H. Denzinger and K. Rahner, trans. R.J. Deferrari (St. Louis, MO: B. Herder Book Co., 1954), 190; 481 [DS 902].

14   Congregation for the Doctrine of the Faith, *Letter on Certain Questions Concerning Eschatology*, May 17, 1979.

15   Thomas Aquinas, *Quaestio disputata de unione Verbi incarnati* art. 1, ad 16, trans. Daniel D. De Haan and Brandon Dahm, "Thomas Aquinas on Separated Souls as Incomplete Human Persons," *The Thomist* 83 (2019): 589-637, particularly 601, no. 32.

16   See Uldrich Zwingli, *Huldrych Zwingli Writings, Vol. One: The Defense of the Reformed Faith*, Pittsburgh Theological Monographs (Eugene,

OR: Pickwick Publications, 1984), 173; Eric Svendson, *Evangelical Answers: A Critique of Current Roman Catholic Apologists* (Lidenhurst, New York: Reformation Press, 1999),158-160.

17 See Michael Hobart Seymour, *Mornings Among the Jesuits at Rome* (London: Seeley, 1852), 145; Jordan Cooper, "A Further Critique of Offering Prayers to the Saints," https://www.youtube.com/watch?v=cf3T3weOjUI.

18 Jerome, *Against Vigilantius* in *St. Jerome: Letters and Select Works*, vol. 6, eds. P. Schaff and H. Wace, trans. W. H. Fremantle, G. Lewis, and W.G. Martley (Christian Literature Company, 1893), 419.

19 See Matt Slick, "Is Praying to the Saints Biblical?", Dec. 6, 2008, Christian Apologetics and Research Ministry (CARM), https://carm.org/roman-catholicism/is-praying-to-the-saints-biblical.

20 See G.K. Beale, *The Book of Revelation: A Commentary on the Greek Text*, The New International Greek Testament Commentary (Grand Rapids, MI; Eerdmans, 1999), 357.

21 For a Protestant who makes the argument that these "prayers" are praises and not petitions, see Slick, "Is Praying to the Saints Biblical?"

22 "Petition addressed to deity, prayer." *A Greek-English Lexicon of the New Testament and Other Early Christian Literature*, 3rd ed., eds. Frederick W. Danker, Walter Bauer, William F. Arndt, and F. Wilbur Gingrich (Chicago: University of Chicago Press, 2000), 878.

23 See *A Greek-English Lexicon of the New Testament and Other Early Christian Literature*, 27, 357, 408.

24 Hermas, *The Shepherd*, bk. 3, simil. 5, ch. 4, https://www.newadvent.org/fathers/02013.htm.

25 Clement of Alexandria, *Miscellanies* (The Stromata), bk. 7, ch. 12, https://www.newadvent.org/fathers/02107.htm.

26 Origen, Prayer 11, quoted in "What the Early Church Believed: The Intercession of the Saints," https://www.catholic.com/tract/the-intercession-of-the-saints.

27 Cyprian of Carthage, Epistles 56.5, https://www.newadvent.org/fathers/050656.htm.

28 Much of our summary is adapted from C. Bernard Ruffin, *Padre Pio: The True Story*, 3rd edition (Huntington, IN: Our Sunday Visitor, 2018).

29 See Fr. Paolino Rossi, "After Much Study, a Miracle," Catholic Culture, https://www.catholicculture.org/culture/library/view.cfm?recnum=1018.

30 See ibid.

31 Quoted in Maryann Gogniat Eidemiller, "The Miracle that Will Make Archbishop Fulton Sheen 'Blessed,'" Our Sunday Visitor, Jul. 22, 2019, https://osvnews.com/2019/07/22/the-miracle-that-will-make-archbishop-fulton-sheen-blessed.

32 See Emma Green, "A Miracle in Peoria?", *The Atlantic*, Mar. 7, 2014, https://www.theatlantic.com/national/archive/2014/03/a-miracle-in-peoria/284304.

33 See Robert Spitzer, "Contemporary Scientifically Validated Miracles Associated with Blessed Mary, Saints and the Holy Eucharist," Magis Center, Sep. 28, 2017, https://f.hubspotusercontent40.net/hubfs/7693347/Contemporary-Scientifically-Validated-Miracles-Associated-with-Blessed-Mary-Saints-and-the-Holy-Eucharist.pdf.

34 See Congregation for the Causes of Saints, "Promulgazione di Decreti della Congregazione delle Cause dei Santi," Jun. 7, 2019.

35 See Isabella Cota, "Woman heard 'be not afraid' before cure sealing John Paul II's sainthood," Reuters, Jul. 5, 2013, https://www.reuters.com/article/us-vatican-johnpaul-costarica/woman-heard-be-not-afraid-before-cure-sealing-john-paul-iis-sainthood-idUSBRE9640WP20130705.

36 See ibid.

37 See Phillip Pullela, "Costa Rican 'miracle' woman was key to John Paul's sainthood," Reuters, Apr. 24, 2014, https://www.reuters.com/article/uk-pope-saints-miracle/costa-rican-miracle-woman-was-key-to-john-pauls-sainthood-idUKBREA3N1P920140424.

38   See Pepe Alonso, "Mora's Miracle: The Costa Rican Woman Who Was Healed Through John Paul II's Intercession," *National Catholic Register*, https://www.ncregister.com/news/mora-s-miracle-the-costa-rican-woman-who-was-healed-through-john-paul-ii-s-intercession.

39   See Cota, "Woman heard 'be not afraid.'"

40   See Alonso, "Mora's Miracle."

41   See Michelle Miller, "Mother Teresa's Miracles: How she Was Declared a Saint," Magis Center, Sep. 5, 2022, https://www.magiscenter.com/blog/mother-teresas-miracles-how-she-was-declared-a-saint.

42   See Sara Kettler, "Mother Teresa: The Miracles That Made Her a Saint," *Biography*, Oct. 14, 2020, https://www.biography.com/religious-figures/mother-teresa-miracles-saint.

43   See Luke Harding and Philip Willan, "Mother Teresa's 'miracle,'" *The Guardian*, Aug. 18, 2001, https://www.theguardian.com/world/2001/aug/19/philipwillan.lukeharding.

44   See Poulomi Banerjee, "Mother's First Miracle: Monica Besra on How She was Cured," *Hindustan Times*, Sep. 3, 2016, https://www.hindustantimes.com/india-news/mother-s-first-miracle-monica-besra-on-how-she-was-cured/story-4UFYt5hycBYuzFpl8aC7oJ.html.

45   See Laurie Goodstein, "How a Priest Made the Case for Mother Teresa's Sainthood," *New York Times*, Aug. 13, 2016, https://www.nytimes.com/2016/08/14/world/europe/mother-teresas-sainthood-priest.html. See also Harding and Willan, "Mother Teresa's 'miracle.'"

46   See Harding and Willan, "Mother Teresa's 'miracle.'"

47   See Kettler, "Mother Teresa." See also Banerjee, "Mother's First Miracle."

48   See Harding and Willan, "Mother Teresa's 'miracle.'"

49   See ibid.

50   See NDTV, "'A Ray Cured Tumor,' Says Woman Who Claimed Mother Teresa's First Miracle," https://www.youtube.com/watch?v=zW6GRVyneww&t=7s.

51   See Jayatri Nag, "'Miracle Woman' Monica Besra Will Celebrate Mother Teresa's Sainthood at Home," *Mumbai Mirror*, Sep. 4, 2016, https://mumbaimirror.indiatimes.com/news/india/miracle-woman-monica-besra-will-celebrate-mother-teresas-sainthood-at-home/articleshow/53999389.cms.

52   See Banerjee, "Mother's First Miracle."

53   Jordan Cooper, a Lutheran pastor and professor of systematic theology, comments on this passage: "The saints in heaven pray for the church and I'm sure they do. Why wouldn't they? But that does not give us precedent ourselves to reason from that . . . and know that they hear us." See Cooper, "A Further Critique of Offering Prayers to the Saints." See also Matt Slick, "Can Mary Hear Our Prayers?", Jun. 10, 2016, CARM, https://carm.org/roman-catholicism/can-mary-hear-our-prayers.

54   Brian Davies, *Thinking About God* (Eugene, OR: Wipd & Stock, 2010), 319.

55   Council of Trent, Session 25, "On the Invocation, Veneration, and Relics, of Saints, and on Sacred Images," 233, emphasis added.

56   Westminster Confession, 1646, "Of the Holy Scripture," sec. 6, https://www.pcaac.org/wp-content/uploads/2022/04/WCFScripureProofs2022.pdf, emphasis added.

57   This line of argumentation is taken from Dave Armstrong, "Biblical Evidence for the Communion of Saints" (Dave Armstrong, 2012), ch. 4.

58   There is some debate over the dating of the prayer, but there's enough scholarly support for the early dating that makes it reasonable to affirm. See Frederica Mathewes-Green, *The Lost Gospel of Mary: The Mother of Jesus in Three Ancient Texts* (Brewster, MA: Paraclete Press, 2007), 85-87. Orthodox scholar Serafim Seppälä concludes that "there are no determinate theological or philological reasons to reject the third-century dating." Serafim Seppälä, *Elämän Äiti. Neitsyt Maria varhaiskristillisessä teologiassa* [*Mother of Life. Virgin*

Mary in Early Christian Theology] (Helsinki: Maahenki, 2010), 84. The third-century dating of the hymn is provided by papyrologist E. Lobel, who dated the papyrus containing the hymn (*Rylands Papyrus* 470) to the third century. See *Catalogue of the Greek and Latin Papyri in the John Rylands Library Manchester*, vol. III, ed. C.H. Roberts (Manchester: Manchester University Press, 1938), 46. C.H. Roberts dates the hymn to the fourth century. For a defense of the earlier dating, see Joe Heschmeyer, "What the Earliest Recorded Marian Prayer Reveals About the Early Church," *Shameless Popery*, http://shamelesspopery.com/sub-tuum. Scholar Hans Förster gives the latest date for the hymn, putting it to the eighth century. See Förster, "Die älteste marianische Antiphon—eine Fehldatierung? Überlegungen zum 'ältesten Beleg' des Sub tuum praesidium" in *Journal of Coptic Studies* 7 (2005): 99–109. But this theory was debunked when the hymn was found in the Georgian Ladgari (chant book) of Jerusalem, proving that the hymn was in liturgical use in the fifth century. See *The First Christian Hymnal: The Songs of the Ancient Jerusalem Church*, 1st ed., trans. Stephen J. Shoemaker (Provo, Utah: Brigham Young University, 2019), xxviii.

59   *Christian Inscriptions*, trans. H.P.V. Nunn (New York: The Macmillan Company, 1920), 16 [no. 29].

60   See "Asking the Prayers of the Saints Peter and Paul," *Silouan*, Jul. 12, 2021, https://silouanthompson.net/2021/07/peter-and-paul. See also Shawn Tribe, "Notes on the Archeology, Relics and Early Roman Christian Devotion to Ss. Peter and Paul," *Liturgical Arts Journal*, Jun. 29, 2021, https://www.liturgicalartsjournal.com/2021/06/notes-on-archeology-relics-and-roman.html; Danilo Mazzoleni, "Ancient Graffiti in Roman Catacombs," *L'Osservatore Romano*, Feb. 6, 2000, https://www.ewtn.com/catholicism/library/ancient-graffiti-in-roman-catacombs-1642.

61   Methodius, Oration on Simeon and Anna 14, https://www.newadvent.org/fathers/0627.htm.

62   Cyril of Jerusalem, Catechetical Lectures 23:9, https://www.newadvent.org/fathers/310123.htm.

63   Ephraim the Syrian, Commentary on Mark, quoted in "What the Early Church Believed: The Intercession of the Saints," https://www.catholic.com/tract/the-intercession-of-the-saints.

64 Gregory of Nazianzen, Orations 18:4, https://www.newadvent.org/fathers/310218.htm.

65 John Chrysostom, Homilies on Second Corinthians 26:2:5, https://www.newadvent.org/fathers/220226.htm.

66 See Norman L. Geisler and Ralph E. MacKenzie, *Roman Catholics and Evangelicals: Agreements and Differences* (Grand Rapids, MI: Baker Academic, 1995), 319, 352; John R. Waiss and James G. McCarthy, *Letters Between a Catholic and an Evangelical: From Debate to Dialogue on the Issues That Separate Us* (Eugene, OR: Harvest House Publishers, 2003), 278; Kenneth J. Colins and Jerry L. Walls, *Roman But Not Catholic: What Remains at Stake 500 Years after the Reformation* (Ada, MI: Baker Academic, 2017), 311. Although it doesn't explicitly refer to 1 Timothy 2:5, the Augsburg Confession makes a similar argument, stating, "Scripture does not teach calling on the saints or pleading for help from them. For it sets before us Christ alone as mediator, atoning sacrifice, high priest, and intercessor." See *The Augsburg Confession*, Article XXI, in *The Book of Concord: The Confessions of the Evangelical Lutheran Church*, eds. Robert Kolb, Timothy J. Wengert, and Charles P. Arand (Minneapolis, MN: Fortress Press, 2000), 59.

67 Jordan Cooper, "A Critique of Prayer to the Saints," https://www.youtube.com/watch?v=3046OcXloZU.

68 Ibid.

69 See Lynda Howard-Munro, *A Rebuttal to Catholic Apologetics* (Mustang, OK: Tate Publishing, 2013), 163.

70 See Akin, *A Daily Defense*, 150.

71 James White, *Answers to Catholic Claims: A Discussion of Biblical Authority* (New York: Crowne Publications, 1990), ch. 9, Kindle edition.

72 This line of reasoning is taken from Jimmy Akin in "Speaking with the Dead? Visions, Apparitions, Saints, Spirits, Ghosts, Prayer, Intercession, Mediums, Seances, Necromancy," *Jimmy Akin's Mysterious World*, Episode 270, Apr. 8, 2023.

73 Protestant apologist Gavin Ortlund makes the argument this way:

"Our concern is that this is a historical accretion, a historical innovation. Something that gradually comes into the picture and not authentically related to the first century and *biblical instruction* and Jesus' teaching." Gavin Ortlund, "Praying to the Saints: A Protestant Critique," https://www.youtube.com/watch?v=TQRQ-bbmVvI, emphasis added. See also Article XXI of the Augsburg Confession: "Scripture does not teach calling on the saints or pleading for help from them." Augsburg Confession, "Of the Worship of the Saints," Article XXI, trans. R. Kolb, T. Wengert, and C. Arand (Minneapolis: Augsburg Fortress, 2000).

74   See Geisler and MacKenzie, *Roman Catholics and Evangelicals*, 188; Ron Rhodes, *Reasoning from the Scriptures with Catholics* (Eugene, OR: Harvest House Publishers, 2000), 79-80.

75   Clement of Rome, First Letter to the Corinthians, ch. 44, https://www.newadvent.org/fathers/1010.htm.

76   Irenaeus, *Against Heresies* III:3:1, https://www.newadvent.org/fathers/0103303.htm.

77   See "How does Protestantism defend the adoption of practices and beliefs not found in the Bible?", https://christianity.stackexchange.com/questions/62203/how-does-protestantism-defend-the-adoption-of-practices-and-beliefs-not-found-in.

78   West Minster Confession of Faith, I.6.

79   The Church of Christ excludes instruments from their workshop services. See Robert Dodson, "Why Does the Church of Christ Not Use Mechanical Instruments of Music in Worship?", *Northwest Church of Christ*, https://www.northwestcofc.org/why-does-the-church-of-christ-not-use-mechanical-instruments-of-music-in-worship.html#:~:text=The%20reason%20we%20do%20not,a%20mechanical%20instrument%20of%20music.

80   Tony Miano and Matt Slick, "Is the Sinner's Prayer Biblical or Not?", CARM, accessed Jul. 19, 2017. The article is no longer available online at its original source. However, it is reproduced here: http://goeagles2u.blogspot.com/2014/06/is-sinners-prayer-biblical-or-not-by.html. I am grateful to Trent Horn for this example. See Trent Horn, "Protestant Traditions You Won't Find in the Bible," Catholic Answers, Nov. 16, 2017, https://www.catholic.com/

magazine/online-edition/protestant-traditions-you-wont-find-in-the-bible. Matt Slick has published a more recent take on this issue with a bit more nuance, affirming that the "Sinner's Prayer" is not in the Bible *per se*, but there are some things in the Bible that justify a sinner receiving Christ. See Matt Slick, "What is the Sinner's Prayer and is it Biblical?", CARM, Aug. 11, 2023, https://carm.org/about-prayer/what-is-the-sinners-prayer-and-is-it-biblical.

81   [The Shepherd said:] "But those who are weak and slothful in prayer hesitate to ask anything from the Lord; but the Lord is full of compassion, and gives without fail to all who ask him. But you, [Hermas,] *having been strengthened by the holy angel [you saw], and having obtained from him such intercession*, and not being slothful, why do you not ask understanding of the Lord, and receive it from him?" Hermas, *The Shepherd* 3:5:4 (A.D. 80), in Jimmy Akin, *The Fathers Know Best: Your Essential Guide to the Teachings of the Early Church* (El Cajon: Catholic Answers, 2010), ch. 52, Kindle edition.

82   See Ortlund, "Praying to the Saints." See also Cooper, "A Further Critique of Offering Prayers to the Saints."

83   I am grateful to Trent Horn for this line of response. See Trent Horn, "REBUTTING Gavin Ortlund on relics and venerating the saints," *Counsel of Trent*, https://www.youtube.com/watch?v=udT_CxDh7MQ.

84   Baptist scholar Gary Shogren states the following: "Copies of books were expensive, even if you could read; this leads Harnack to conclude that 'for a considerable period of time [private reading] was somewhat infrequent, simply because of the lack of copies. This explains why mention is never made of the private reading in the New Testament, nor in the Didache or in the Epistle of Barnabas' (Harnack, p. 33). So for the great majority of Christians, Bible study between meetings would mean, reviewing and rehearsing what you heard on Sunday and perhaps memorized." Gary Shogren, "The Public Reading of Scripture in the Early Church in the Church of Today," Open Our Eyes, Lord, https://openoureyeslord.com/2021/05/08/the-public-reading-of-scripture-in-the-early-church-in-the-church-of-today.

85   See Paul James-Griffiths, "The Church Fathers on Musical Instruments," Christian Heritage Edinburgh, Aug. 20, 2016, https://www.christianheritageedinburgh.org.uk/2016/08/20/the-church-

fathers-on-musical-instruments.

86 "And even if you wish to sing and play to the harp or lyre, there is no blame. You shall imitate the righteous Hebrew king in his thanksgiving to God." Clement of Alexandria, Instructor, bk. 2, ch. 4, https://www.newadvent.org/fathers/02092.htm.

87 "[There is a] high view of honoring him [Polycarp], but [it] makes a distinction: 'We worship Christ as the Son of God; the martyrs, however, we love as disciples and imitators of the Lord, as is right, on account of their unsurpassable benevolence toward their King and Teacher; and we wish to become their companions and disciples.' No prayers to Polycarp. I don't see this practice early on." Ortlund, "Praying to the Saints."

88 "When you're looking at Irenaeus fighting against the Gnostics, because that's the kind of place where you may expect to see it, to say, 'Oh, no it's not true,' that there are these kind of intermediary beings in that way, but we do have the saints, who are these kind of co-mediators in some sense, and we can pray to them and work through them. He doesn't do that in the places where you would expect him to do that." Cooper, "A Further Critique of Offering Prayers to the Saints."

89 See also paragraphs 519, 739, 1341, 1361, 1369, 2593, and 2635.

90 See Ortlund, "Praying to the Saints."

91 Ortlund appeals to similar invocations that were appealed to at Nicaea II. See Gavin Ortlund, "Venerating Icons: A Protestant Critique," Truth Unites, https://www.youtube.com/watch?v=AkNuganI0JA.

92 See Cooper, "A Critique of Prayer to the Saints."

93 *Latdict*, "venerari," https://latin-dictionary.net/definition/38505/veneror-venerari-veneratus.

94 Second Council of Nicaea, *The Decree of the Holy, Great, Ecumenical Synod, Second of Nicea*, in *Nicene and Post-Nicene Fathers of the Christian Church: Volume XIV, The Seven Ecumenical Councils*, eds. P. Schaff and H. Wace, trans. H.R. Percival (New York: Charles Scribner's Sons, 1900), 550.

THE SAINTS PRAY FOR YOU

95   Council of Trent, "On the Invocation," 234-235.

96   *A Greek-English Lexicon of the New Testament and Other Early Christian Literature*, 280.

97   Council of Trent, "On the Invocation," 234-235.

98   James White, *The Roman Catholic Controversy: Catholics and Protestants—Do the Differences Still Matter?* (Minneapolis, MN: Bethany House Publishers, 1996), 211.

99   *Greek-English Lexicon*, 882.

100 See Jimmy Akin, *Chosen by God: God's Elect in the Bible and Early Christian Writings* (Critical Insight, 2019).

101 See Ortlund, "Praying to the Saints"; Cooper, "A Further Critique of Offering Prayers to the Saints."

102 The *Heidelberg Catechism*, a compilation of Calvinist doctrine, states that the invocation of the saints contravenes the First Commandment. Question 94 states, "What does God require in the first commandment?" Answer: "That, on peril of my soul's salvation, I avoid and flee all idolatry, sorcery, enchantments, invocation of saints or of other creatures; and that I rightly acknowledge the only true God, trust in Him alone." *Heidelberg Catechism*, 2011, Question 94, https://web.archive.org/web/20210415104958/http://www.rcus.org/heidelberg-catechism-2011.

103 See Cooper, "A Further Critique of Offering Prayers to the Saints." James White makes the same kind of argument: "Prayer, it is asserted [in Scripture], is an act of worship, and we are to worship God alone." White, *Answers to Catholic Claims*, ch. 9.

104 See Jimmy Akin, "What Does the Church Actually Say About 'Praying to the Saints'?", Dec. 25, 2020, http://jimmyakin.com/2020/12/what-does-the-church-actually-say-about-praying-to-the-saints.html.

105 See Akin, *Chosen by God*.

106 *Latdict*, "cultus," https://latin-dictionary.net/search/latin/cultus.

107   See Ortlund, "Praying to the Saints"; Cooper, "A Further Critique of Offering Prayers to the Saints."

108   Ludwig Ott, *Fundamentals of Catholic dogma* (B. Herder Book Company, 1957), 320.

109   John Damascene, *An Exact Exposition of the Orthodox Faith*, ch. 16, in *Nicene and Post-Nicene Fathers of the Christian Church: Volume IX, St. Hilary of Poitiers, John of Damascus*, eds. P. Schaff and H. Wace, trans. S.D.F. Salmond (Buffalo, NY: Christian Literature Company, 1899), 88.

110   I am grateful to Trent Horn for this line of reasoning. See Trent Horn, "REBUTTING Gavin Ortlund on Icons (with Jimmy Akin)," *The Counsel of Trent Podcast*, https://www.youtube.com/watch?v=v0I33o_GA1M.

111   See ibid.

112   This line of reasoning is taken from Jimmy Akin in Horn's podcast video rebutting Ortlund's critique of icons. See ibid.

113   This example is taken from Dave Armstrong, *Biblical Evidence for the Communion of Saints* (Dave Armstrong, 2012), ch. 10.

114   I am grateful to Trent Horn for this line of argumentation. See Horn, "REBUTTING Gavin Ortlund on Icons." The nature of the kiss being a fraternal kiss on the lips is at least how the second- and third-century Christians practiced it. See Michael Phillip Pen, "A Brief History of the Christian Ritual Kiss," *Church Life Journal*, https://churchlifejournal.nd.edu/articles/a-brief-history-of-the-christian-ritual-kiss.

115   See Ortlund, "Venerating Icons."

116   Ibid.

117   See Geisler and MacKenzie, *Roman Catholics and Evangelicals*, 321-322, 325-326; Waiss and McCarthy, *Letters Between a Catholic and an Evangelical*, 278.

118   See also Akin, *A Daily Defense*, 43.

119 Leviticus 26:1 is another text appealed to, which says almost exactly the same thing as Exodus 20:5. See Ortlund, "Venerating Icons."

120 I am grateful to Jimmy Akin for this description of the "limits" of God's commands. See Horn, "REBUTTING Gavin Ortlund on Icons."

121 See Ortlund, "Venerating Icons."

122 This response is inspired by Jimmy Akin's response to Ortlund on this issue. See Horn, "REBUTTING Gavin Ortlund on Icons."

123 Council of Trent, "On the Invocation," 234-235.

124 Ortlund, "Venerating Icons."

125 See Lynn Martin, "Early Church Fathers on Icons," https:// anabaptistfaith.org/church-fathers-icons; Ortlund, "Venerating Icons."

126 For an in-depth treatment of this issue, see Horn, "REBUTTING Gavin Ortlund on Icons."

127 See Ortlund, "Venerating Icons."

128 Justin Martyr, First Apology, ch. 9, in *The Ante-Nicene Fathers: Volume I, The Apostolic Fathers with Justin Martyr and Irenaeus*, eds. A. Roberts, J. Donaldson, & A. C. Coxe (Buffalo, NY: Christian Literature Company, 1885), 165.

129 Irenaeus, *Against Heresies*, bk. I, ch. 25, no. 6, in *The Apostolic Fathers*, vol. 1, 351.

130 Hippolytus, *The Refutation of All Heresies*, bk. 7, ch. 20, in *The Ante-Nicene Fathers: Volume V Fathers of the Third Century: Hippolytus, Cyprian, Novatian, Appendix*, trans. J.H. MacMahon, eds. A. Roberts, J. Donaldson, & A.C. Coxe (Buffalo, NY: Christian Literature Company, 1886), 114.

131 This interpretation is offered by Horn in his online video, "REBUTTING Gavin Ortlund on Icons."

132 "This idea has raised them to such a pitch of pride, that some of them declare themselves similar to Jesus; while others, still more

mighty, maintain that they are superior to his disciples, such as Peter and Paul, and the rest of the apostles, whom they consider to be in no respect inferior to Jesus." Irenaeus, *Against Heresies*, bk. 1, ch. 25, no.2.

133 I am grateful to Tim Staples for this response. See Tim Staples, *Friends in High Places*, CD set (El Cajon, CA: Catholic Answers).

134 Clement of Alexandria, *Stromata*, bk. 5, ch. 5, in *The Ante-Nicene Fathers: Volume II, Fathers of the Second Century: Hermas, Tatian, Athenagoras, Theophilus, and Clement of Alexandria*, vol. 2, eds. A. Roberts, J. Donaldson, & A.C. Coxe (Buffalo, NY: Christian Literature Company, 1885), 451.

135 Id., 530.

136 See Martin, "Early Church Fathers on Icons."

137 Encyclical Epistle of the Church at Smyrna, ch. 18, in *The Ante-Nicene Fathers: Volume I, The Apostolic Fathers with Justin Martyr and Irenaeus*, eds. A. Roberts, J. Donaldson, and A.C. Coxe (Buffalo, NY: Christian Literature Company, 1885), 43.

138 John Chrysostom, *Homily on St. Ignatius*, in *Nicene and Post-Nicene Fathers: Volume IX, Saint Chrysostom: On the Priesthood, Ascetic Treatises, Select Homilies and Letters, Homilies on the Statues*, trans. W.R.W. Stephens and T.P. Brandram, ed. P. Schaff (Buffalo, NY: Christian Literature Company, 1889), 140.

139 Athanasius of Alexandria, *Life of Antony*, in *Nicene and Post-Nicene Fathers: Volume IV, St. Athanasius: Select Works and Letters*, trans. H. Ellershaw Jr., eds. P. Schaff and H. Wace (New York: Christian Literature Company, 1892), 220.

140 Basil of Caesarea, Letter 49, in *Nicene and Post-Nicene Fathers: Volume VIII, St. Basil: Letters and Select Works*, trans. B. Jackson, eds. P. Schaff and H. Wace (New York: Christian Literature Company, 1895), 153.

141 Id., Letter 155, 210.

142 Id., Letter 197, 235.

143 Jerome, *Against Vigilantius*, in *Nicene and Post-Nicene Fathers: Volume*

VI, St. Jerome: Letters and Select Works, trans. W.G. Martley, eds. P. Schaff and H. Wace (New York: Christian Literature Company, 1893), 418.

144 Id., 419.

145 Id., 421.

146 Cooper, "A Critique of Prayer to the Saints."

147 Ortlund, "Relics: A Protestant Critique," https://www.youtube.com/watch?v=i5vm_nSWnko&t=19s.

148 Cooper, "A Critique of Prayer to the Saints."

149 Ortlund, "Relics: A Protestant Critique."

150 See Trent Horn, "Convert Your Protestant Friend with Miracles," Catholic Answers, May 15, 2023, https://www.catholic.com/magazine/online-edition/miracles-keep-going-and-going.

151 Ortlund, "Relics."

152 Council of Trent, "On the Invocation."

153 Ortlund, "Relics."

154 Fourth Lateran Council, "Regarding Saints' Relics," Constitution 62. Available online at https://www.papalencyclicals.net/councils/ecum12-2.htm.

155 I am grateful to Trent Horn for this line of response and research. See Horn, "REBUTTING Gavin Ortlund on relics and venerating the saints."

156 The Nazareth Inscription, trans. Clyde E. Billington, quoted in Billington, "The Shiloh Excavations," Associates for Biblical Research, https://biblearchaeology.org/research/new-testament-era/4658-the-nazareth-inscription-proof-of-the-resurrection-of-christ.

157 Charles Freeman, *Holy Bones, Holy Dust: How Relics Shaped the History of Medieval Europe* (New Haven: Yale University Press, 2011), 5.

158   Ortlund, "Relics."

159   "Patron Saints," *The Catholic Encyclopedia*, https://www.newadvent.
       org/cathen/11562a.htm.

160   Irenaeus, *Against Heresies*, bk. 5, ch. 19, https://www.newadvent.org/
       fathers/0103519.htm.

161   Methodius of Olympus, Oration on Simeon and Anna, ch. 14,
       https://www.newadvent.org/fathers/0627.htm.

162   See John Paul II, Apostolic Letter Proclaiming St. Thérèse a Doctor
       of the Church *Divini Amoris Scientia* (Oct. 19, 1997).

163   See Leo XIII, Encyclical on the Restoration of Christian Philosophy
       Aeterni Patris (Aug. 4, 1879).

164   "By the inspiration of the Holy Spirit, for the honor of the holy
       and undivided Trinity, for the glory and adornment of the virgin
       mother of God, for the exaltation of the Catholic faith, and for
       the furtherance of the Catholic religion, by the authority of Jesus
       Christ our Lord, of the blessed apostles Peter and Paul, and by our
       own: 'We declare, pronounce, and define that the doctrine which
       holds that the most blessed virgin Mary, in the first instance of her
       conception, by a singular grace and privilege granted by almighty
       God, in view of the merits of Jesus Christ, the Savior of the human
       race, was preserved free from all stain of original sin, is a doctrine
       revealed by God and therefore to be believed firmly and constantly
       by all the faithful." Pius IX, Apostolic Constitution Defining the
       Immaculate Conception *Ineffabilis Deus* (Dec. 8, 1854).

165   Thomas Aquinas, *Responsio de 43 articulis* 2-3.

166   Congregation for the Doctrine of the Faith, *The Message of
       Fatima* (Jun. 26, 2000), https://www.vatican.va/roman_curia/
       congregations/cfaith/documents/rc_con_cfaith_doc_20000626_
       message-fatima_en.html.

167   United States Conference of Catholic Bishops, "Popular Devotional
       Practices: Basic Questions and Answers," q. 9, http://www.usccb.
       org/prayer-and-worship/prayers-and-devotions/prayers/popular-
       devotional-practices-basic-questions-andanswers.cfm.

168   See Philip Kosloski, "What is the Six Sundays devotion in honor of St. Aloysius Gonzaga?" *Aleteia*, Jun. 21, 2018, https://aleteia.org/2018/06/21/what-is-the-six-sundays-devotion-in-honor-of-staloysius-gonzaga.